FEED
YOUR
soul

A Cookbook
That Nourishes
Body, Mind and Spirit

George Fowler
Jeff Lehr

A FIRESIDE BOOK
Published by Simon & Schuster
NEW YORK LONDON TORONTO
SYDNEY TOKYO SINGAPORE

FIRESIDE
Rockefeller Center
1230 Avenue of the Americas
New York, New York 10020

First Fireside Edition 1994
Published by arrangement with Tradery House/The Wimmer Companies, Inc.

Manufactured in the United States of America

1   3   5   7   9   10   8   6   4   2

Library of Congress Cataloging-in-Publication Data
Fowler, George.
[Teaching your heart to dance cookbook]
Feed your soul : a cookbook that nourishes body, mind
and spirit/George Fowler, Jeff Lehr.
p.   cm.
Reprint. Originally published 1993 under title:
Teaching your heart to dance cookbook.
"A Fireside book."
Includes index.
1. Cookery(Natural foods).   I. Lehr, Jeff.   II. Title.
TX741.F67   1994
641.5'63—dc20   94-22513
                                                                CIP

ISBN: 0-671-89100-6

Previously titled Teaching Your Heart to Dance Cookbook

TABLE OF CONTENTS

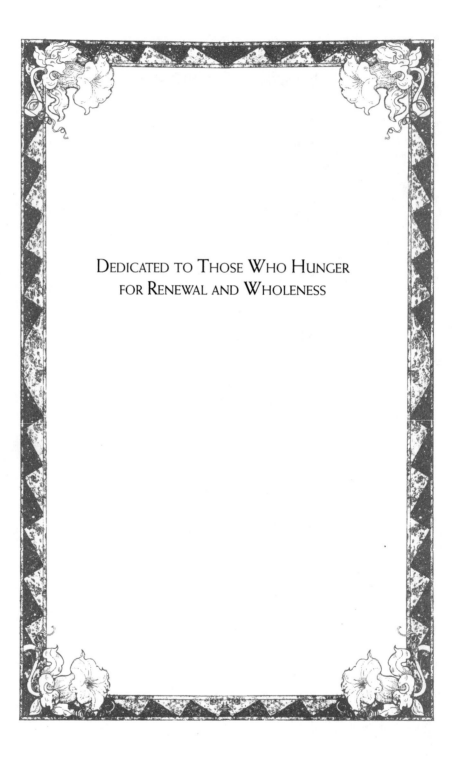

DEDICATED TO THOSE WHO HUNGER
FOR RENEWAL AND WHOLENESS

PROLOGUE

*I*t is significant that at a time when more persons than ever before are realizing the need for enlightened bodily nutrition, many are also moving into a more universal spiritual awareness. For the first time in history, great numbers of people are learning to recognize—and appreciate—both today's reviving of interest in natural cooking and the rediscovery of spirituality at the core of the world's religious cultures.

We have come to understand that the most critically selected and carefully prepared food in the world will not make or keep us healthy and happy if we live in fear, depression, hatred or other negative life circumstances. But, equally, all the right thought and feeling in the world will not keep us healthy—or alive—if we do not provide our bodies with good food. A truly complete human diet and cookbook should address all of our nutritional needs: those of body, heart, mind, and spirit.

We function as holistic units. Food, thought, and feeling serve together to nourish us. The tastiest and most nutritious foods join deep spiritual understanding to enhance each other as they nourish the whole person. This work is built on the premise that there is a nourishing component in spirituality just as there is a spiritual component in food. It marries recipes for responsible, balanced, savory eating with universal spiritual insights that will surround that eating with a sense of ultimate security and unshakable joy.

As suggested by the ethereal nature of its art, this is a quiet book. It is written to provide you a way—a "philosophy"—for preparing natural food and for engaging your spirit while you nourish your whole person.

Author of the Meditative Reflections

GEORGE FOWLER is a writer, lecturer and teacher specializing in spiritual growth. A former Trappist monk and priest for over two decades and holder of several advanced academic degrees, Fowler applies his expertise to help people realize their potential for fulfillment and inner growth within their individual belief systems. After leaving organized religion, Fowler, who is married to a former nun, worked 15 years for the defense industry, first counseling Vietnam returnees and later designing nuclear weapons security. Today, he is a much in-demand newspaper columnist, radio commentator and lecturer on self-empowerment and meditation. Fowler is also founder and director of The National Foundation for Healing Religious Abuse located in Nashville, TN.

Author of the Recipes and Food Axioms

JEFF LEHR's career as a cooking instructor, chef, consultant and lecturer has been inspired by a keen interest in natural foods and nutrition which spans more than 18 years. After completing an apprenticeship at The Seventh Inn in Boston with Japanese master chef Hiroshi Hayashi in 1979, he moved to Memphis, TN, to help open the area's first full-service natural foods restaurant, LaMontagne, where he worked as chef and kitchen manager for 9 years. His cooking classes for Squash Blossom Market and regional health-care facilities have helped many people make the transition to natural and heart-healthy eating habits. His "Food and Wellness" and "Sacredness of Food" seminars help participants explore the multidimensional nature of their relationship with food. Lehr is the founder of Culinary Consulting Associates, which provides various culinary consulting and educational services.

Salads & Dressings

I HONOR THE DIVINITY OF MY PHYSICAL EXISTENCE WITH LOVE
AND RESPECT FOR MY BODY.

As I grow in acceptance and appreciation of my connection with all
Life, I see that my physical self is no less spiritual than any other part
of me. In learning to live this truth, I come to honor, respect and care
for my body, and, as often as possible, offer it the highest quality
nourishment the earth has to offer.

Selecting my food and transforming it into simple, gentle, healing
nourishment can greatly enhance my receptivity to Life by creating a
stronger, healthier and more peaceful personal condition.

SALADS AND DRESSINGS

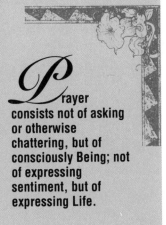
For many of us, a busy schedule is one of the biggest obstacles to eating wholesome, natural foods. Salads provide a wonderful answer to this dilemma. Easily prepared using just about anything you might find in the refrigerator, you can take quick advantage of both store-bought and home-prepared foods. Why be limited by the notion of salad as pale lettuce with a few raw adornments? The possibilities are truly endless: I doubt that I've eaten the same combination of ingredients on a salad twice in the last year!

Whether eaten as a part of a meal or as the meal itself, salads are a great way to consume fresh vegetables to balance the heavier foods we eat. Lemon or natural vinegar helps add the essential flavor of "sour" to our nourishment. Try eating salads which emphasize raw or barely cooked vegetables more often in the spring or summer, or when your body feels the need for "cleansing". In cooler weather, go for the heartier, cooked ingredients, and smaller, or less frequent, raw salads. Experiment for yourself, to see what feels best to your body. While you're at it, let your spirit enjoy the rewards of creating visually pleasing, colorful arrangements using nature's palette!

FAST FOOD

For those busy times when your vegetable needs might take a back seat to other priorities, and you don't want to wash a single dish.

1	small	carrot
1	medium	stalk celery
		-or-
1	small wedge	green cabbage
1		red radish
		-or-
	1-inch	chunk of daikon radish

Peel or trim off dried or discolored spots, scrub well, then slip them into a plastic bag and take 'em with you. Chew well. Notice how it feels.

Yield: Good balance for your heavier sustenance

A SIMPLE SALAD

Though a salad may consist of almost any food, the kind my body seems to like the best is one of fresh, deep-green leafy vegetables. The greener, the better. I feel lighter, "cleaner", somehow clearer-headed after a meal of mostly leafy greens or lettuces, especially at midday. They are said to have a cleansing, de-toxifying effect. For those who don't tolerate the lettuce family well, there are many other vegetables which can joyfully take their place.

The quantities given are for one serving, and are guidelines only; use your judgement. And keep in mind: sometimes the best salads have the fewest ingredients!

1-2	cups	one or more mild leafy salad greens
¼-1	cup	bitter or pungent greens
	just a wee bit	otherwise strongly-flavored greens
¼ to ½	cup	something of color or crunch
2	tablespoons	
	to ½ cup	something of substance, to balance the rest (optional)
1 - 4	tablespoons	your favorite dressing

Carefully wash and trim all the vegetables, removing any bruised or wilted parts. The greens may be washed individually or briefly submerged in several changes of cold water, allowing any soil or sand to sink before lifting the greens out slowly without disturbing the water. Use a salad spinner or cotton pillowcase to spin-dry the greens before serving to allow dressing to cling to them. They'll keep longer in the refrigerator, too. Arrange the greens on your plate in a way that is pleasing to you. Store the rest in a sealed bag or container in the refrigerator for up to three days.

Grate, shred, slice or dice the ingredients to your liking (the flowers are best left whole). Arrange them on the greens, with beiges and whites beneath the more colorful choices, or any way you like.

Top with items of substance, if used.

Add the dressing, take time to give thanks and slow down before eating.

Yield: A grateful body and soul

*I*n ancient times an idea was prevalent that kings ruled by divine right. God had given them their thrones, it was said, and to oppose a ruler was to oppose God. Much could be asked about the shaky wisdom of such an endorsement of the absolute power that many monarchs assumed, but the idea does make a point for us today. Ask yourself if you really feel, in your heart of hearts, at the core of your thinking, that you are completely and wholeheartedly backed up and supported, loved and forever embraced by the one you know as God. You have a divine right and endorsement in ways that were never claimed for king or emperor. If you haven't realized this, you have a wonderful surprise in store for you as you ponder the meditations in this book.

SIMPLE SALAD OPTIONS

There was a time when people believed that only a shaman, saint or otherwise apparently exceptional person was invited to have high spiritual experience. Many still believe this today. The truth of the matter is that those specially blessed persons in past ages were but modeling what the world's sacred writings state to be the common condition of—and invitation to—every single human being. You cannot remind yourself often enough that you are, yourself, personally and right now, invited to the most exciting and sublime adventure of all: a *conscious* experience of Eternal Being. After you have begun to have this experience, you will be led to something that is greater still. This Being is with you at every instant and is not precisely present *in* you, but is, rather, present *as* you.

Mild leafy salad greens	lettuces: greenleaf, butterhead, Bibb, romaine, redleaf, oakleaf, iceberg, and others: spinach, Belgian, endive, Chinese cabbage, alfalfa sprouts, buckwheat sprouts
Bitter or pungent greens	dandelion, escarole, curly endive, parsley, wild lettuce, arugula, roquette or rocket, nasturtium leaves, watercress, wild cress, green cabbage, baby mustard greens, sprouts of sunflower or radish
Otherwise strongly-flavored greens	cilantro or Chinese parsley, sorrel, chickweed, wild violet, scallions, wild onion, garlic or chives, dillweed, basil, oregano, tarragon, mint, fennel or anise leaves, marjoram
Something of color or crunch	carrot, beet, radicchio, red cabbage, celery, cauliflower, turnip, Jerusalem artichoke, vine-ripened tomatoes, red or gold bell pepper, lightly-cooked winter squash, sweet potatoes or yams, purple onion, fennel or anise, flowers of arugula, redbud, wild blue violet, radish, mustard, borage, rose (be sure it's unsprayed), nasturtium, pansies, red clover
Something of substance	whole grain croutons, tofu or cooked beans, cooked whole grain or pasta, roasted or soaked nuts or seeds, a bit of cheese, cooked natural poultry or meat, or cooked seafood harvested with care from clean waters

FRUITS OF SUMMER SALAD

Here's an idea for a quick, delicious and beautiful breakfast that is light, cleansing and energizing. Though raw fruit is said to digest most easily when eaten alone, soaking the optional nuts overnight apparently renders them more compatible, and their (highly unsaturated) fat content helps this meal stay with you throughout the morning. Feasting on fresh, fiber-rich, nutrient-dense and sweet complex carbohydrates helps to keep me from craving the empty-calorie sweets that put my health in jeopardy. Experiment with this as an alternative to your usual (or lack of) breakfast and see how it feels.

1	large	fresh, ripe peach
		-or-
1		orange
2	small	ripe kiwi fruit
¼-½	cup	fresh blueberries or other fresh, ripe berries
2	tablespoons	soaked whole almonds or filberts (see below)

Wash peaches and blueberries; peel kiwi (and orange, if used). Cut peach or orange and kiwi into ½" slices. Layer fruit in a wide, shallow bowl or plate as follows: peaches or oranges first, kiwi slices scattered on top, then blueberries allowed to fall naturally across the others. Garnish with sliced or whole soaked nuts.

Yield: Give thanks, see it nourishing your body, and enjoy!

SOAKED ALMONDS OR HAZELNUTS

When stored properly and left intact, nuts and seeds retain the gift of life. When soaked in water, the forces required for growth are activated; complex starches become more digestible and nutrient content increases as the living seed begins to grow. For whole nuts, the resulting fresh taste and crunchy texture goes well with raw vegetable or dried fruit snacks, hot or cold breakfast cereals and desserts. Their relatively high fat content suggests that they be used sparingly, but consider this: because the "sprouting" process causes the nut to expand, soaked nuts contain 75% of the fat content as the same quantity raw.

½	cup	whole almonds or hazelnuts (filberts)
¾	cup	water

Sort out any broken or damaged nuts; soak 12 hours in water. Drain well and leave at room temperature for 8-12 hours; rinse in cool water twice during this time. Refrigerate for up to 2-3 days.

⅔ cup

---

*G*o out under a starlit sky some late evening and choose for yourself a single star as your companion for the next 24 hours. Any star will do, and don't waste time trying to find out what name or number astronomers have assigned it. You might decide to choose a completely different one the next night. Your purpose is to expand your mind's points of reference, not to satisfy its idle curiosity. Whenever you awaken during the night and frequently in the following day smile as you recall your twinkling—and exploding, roaring— companion in the Universe. It continues with a stability and evenness of purpose that is a model for you. If you do this faithfully, watch how differently, perhaps humorously, you begin to respond to a stubbed toe, a tardy friend, a disappointment or loss. Left to our old habits, we are all unbelievably small-minded and parochial in this Universe of blazing beauty. Stars are good companions.

SALAD OF SPRING GREENS AND FLOWERS

We are blessed to have a backyard where wild violets grow. Each year they show their wonderful faces sometime in mid- to late February: blue-violet flowers nestled among the familiar, heart-shaped, dark green leaves. And when they're most abundant in April and May, we'll welcome another Spring favorite - Redbud blossoms, flourishing again on a young tree rescued from a tangled web of honeysuckle several years ago. Blooming on through the peak of lettuce season, these colorful perennials offer welcome contrast - not only to the greening yard, but also our salad plates! That's right, both are edible, tasty, and nutritious as well. One-half cup of violet flowers contain as much vitamin C as four oranges! Here, they lend their pleasant hues to fresh young greens. A touch of something sweet and orange brings balance.

1	cup	fresh young lettuce (greenleaf, redtip, romaine and/or Bibb)
1	cup	other spring greens (dandelion, violet leaves, arugula)
½	cup	baked or steamed butternut squash, warm or chilled (or shredded carrot)
a	sprinkling of	redbud and/or violet flowers
1	tablespoon	chopped, roasted pecans, walnuts or filberts
1	splash	simple lemon vinaigrette (see p. 20)

Wash lettuces and greens and dry well in salad spinner. Assemble ingredients in order given above, with lettuce on bottom of plate.

Yield: An experience of Joy.

Note: It is best to use caution with wild plants which cannot be positively identified; any uncertainty may be easily cleared up with a visit to the public library or reference room at your local botanic garden. While all blue-colored violets are edible, some yellow species are not.

---

*L*ooked at one way, there are millions of separate rays of the sun shining through openings in the forest canopy and playing on the forest floor. If these rays were to look back to where they originate, however, they would see their reality quite differently. They would realize that they each have their light only by sharing the light of a single source, the sun. They would realize that they shine and exist as part of one light only. They would see that that light was given to them not in some distant past, but is being received anew in each present moment, instant by instant. And so it is when you begin to recognize that you exist and live by sharing the only Existence and Life there is or ever could be, when you realize that you share *the* Existence and that you receive It now—and now—and now— forever.

FIESTA RICE AND CORN SALAD

*Grain salads are a great way to take advantage of "intentional leftovers."
Any cooked grain with a dry, separate-grain texture may be combined with
vegetables, seasonings and salad dressing to create a quick meal. If you're
improvising with leftover cooked vegetables, be sure to add some fresh raw or
crunchy additions, and something with bright color. The jicama (pro-
nounced hic'-ah-muh) used here is a tuber from Central America and
Mexico which has crisp, white, slightly sweet flesh inside its thick, brown
skin. Basmati means "Queen of Fragrance" in India, where this rice originated. You'll see why when you smell and taste it! The white type is not a
whole grain, but its delicate texture is a nice treat!*

3	tablespoons	olive oil
⅓	cup	lime or lemon juice, fresh
¼	cup	fresh cilantro, chopped
2	teaspoons	cumin ground
1	teaspoon	black pepper, ground
¼	teaspoon	sea salt, optional
2	cups	cooked white basmati rice (see A Simple Pot of Rice, Variation #2, p.74)
¼	cup	purple onion, chopped finely
1½	cups	pinto, red or kidney beans, cooked until tender but still firm (see p. 65)
2	cups	corn, cut off the cob in strips
1	cup	tomato, ripe, diced
¼	medium	jicama, peeled and diced, about 1 cup
½	medium	green bell pepper, minced
½	cup	sliced black olives

Combine first six ingredients in a small bowl or jar; stir or
shake well; allow to sit while preparing other ingredients. Mix
remaining ingredients in a large bowl; add dressing. Marinate
for at least 1 hour before serving. Garnish with Spiced Roasted
Pepitas and Sunflower Seeds (see p. 126).

about 6½ cups, 4 to 6 servings

*Quick Variation: Substitute ½ cup bottled vinaigrette dressing for the oil
and lime juice; one 16-ounce can of beans for home-cooked; 10-12 ounces
frozen corn for fresh. Long grain brown rice may be used instead of basmati
rice.*

When a poor person who has been accustomed to a life of poverty and panic finds that all the while he or she has had a pocket filled with priceless gems, all that remains for that person to do is to lighten up and dance! To really get into such light-heartedness, however, such a one must *remember* the new-found riches.

Thoreau said he went to the woods near Walden Pond to learn to live deliberately. To live deliberately is to live consciously, and that is what we are here for. High consciousness, sometimes called enlightenment, is nothing but full consciousness, full awareness deliberately sought and deliberately maintained. You came to this world to learn to live deliberately; *deliberately* conscious, that is.

SACRED SALAD

Protein-rich Quinoa occupied a sacred place in the beliefs of the ancient Incan civilization. Domesticated in the Andean Highlands as long as 5,000 years ago, it is still referred to there as Chisya Mama, or Mother Grain.

This salad is made in a manner similar to Tabouli, the Middle Eastern salad of marinated cracked wheat. Any pre-cooked whole grain may be used this way, provided it has been cooked with the minimum amount of liquid needed to rehydrate it to a fluffy, separate-grain texture. Since cereal grains keep well refrigerated up to 5 days, intentional leftovers can be a source of very quick and easy meals. If you have some pre-cooked pilaf and salad greens on hand, this salad can be ready in 5-10 minutes.

This recipes allows you to use the amount of grain you have on hand. Use your intuition to help you decide on the proportions and quantities; there is no right or wrong. Your version may emphasize cucumber over tomato, or not use it at all; the level of tanginess is definitely a matter of personal preference. It is said that the Incas are an extremely creative culture. May this be their gift to you.

> Savory Quinoa-Vegetable Pilaf, chilled (see p. 76)
> vine-ripened fresh tomato, diced
> cucumber, peeled if waxed, seeds removed and
>   chopped (optional)
> fresh garlic, minced, or scallions, sliced thinly, or
>   purple onion, chopped.
> Simple Lemon Vinaigrette (see p. 20) or your
>   favorite bottled vinaigrette-type dressing
> fresh green lettuce or other salad greens
>   (see A Simple Salad, p. 10)

Combine all ingredients except dressing in a mixing bowl and stir well. Add dressing to taste. Allow to marinate, if possible, for 30 minutes. Serve marinated grain on top of greens.

Quick Variation: Arrange greens on individual plates, then scatter ingredients over top. Add dressing and enjoy!

This may be made with any simply-cooked grain; use what you have on hand.

Don't berate yourself if too often you find that you live compulsively, impulsively or, as it were, half-consciously. Don't berate yourself, but do lovingly keep your sights on living deliberately. Remind yourself that in conscious awareness of Reality you will find all bliss, fulfillment, security, joy, peace and whatever else for which your heart cries out.

If you do not yet experience uninterrupted peace and joy, you still have much awareness waiting for you. And what is the means to that increased awareness? Merely—and only—this: smile and learn to quietly Be. And know that the first thing you must do to "quietly Be" is not to flog yourself for not yet knowing how to quietly be!

SALAD OF SUCCOTASH WITH RED PEPPER VINAIGRETTE

Some salads are born of the need for a quick, one dish meal. If I'd made Red Pepper Garnish for soup and a double batch of succotash a few days earlier, this might be the happy result. Serve warm or chilled.

⅓	cup	Roasted Red Pepper Garnish (see p. 30)
3	tablespoons	Simple Lemon Vinaigrette (see p. 20) or your favorite bottled vinaigrette- type dressing
1	batch	Msiquatash (see p. 52)
4	cups	salad greens, prepared as described in A Simple Salad (see p. 10)
	to taste	freshly-ground black pepper
¼	cup	roasted sunflower seeds

Combine pepper puree with vinaigrette dressing; shake well. Prepare succotash. While succotash cooks, prepare salad greens. Arrange greens on serving plates; top each with 1 cup warm or chilled succotash, then 2 tablespoons of dressing. Add black pepper to taste; garnish with roasted seeds.

Quick Variation: Use bottled French-type dressing to replace Simple Lemon Vinaigrette.

4 servings

*T*he speed with which you come consciously into your inheritance of joy depends on your conscious efforts. This does *not* mean that you should be intensely applied to spiritual striving at every moment. When people do that, spirituality tends to separate them from others and from real life and becomes, rightly, a thing of ridicule. What this counsel does mean is that, quite quietly and peacefully and without drama, you consistently orient your thinking, doing and reacting to habits of peace, lightheartedness and trust and away from anxiety, rush, fear and harsh judgment. The speed of your arrival at joy is proportionate to the consistency with which you do this.

WATERCRESS, SWEET POTATO AND ROASTED PECAN SALAD

This wonderful salad was created on one of those days when I had about 5 minutes to prepare lunch. The potato and pecans had been roasted the day before in An Ovenful of Simple Veggies (see p. 44); the watercress was easy enough to prepare quickly. Substitute lettuce if you must, but the unique, peppery taste and nutritional potency of this crisp, deep green vegetable are unmatched by other commonly available salad greens. It is much higher in calcium, iron, and potassium, as well as vitamins A and C.

If you haven't had sweet squash or potato chilled on a salad, you're in for a treat - the smooth, creamy texture, sweet taste and deep orange color is good balance for dark leafy greens and a simple dressing.

1	bunch	watercress
1	medium	sweet potato or yam, baked, then chilled
a	pinch of	salt
a	squeeze of	lemon juice
a	sprinkle of	canola or extra virgin olive oil
½	cup	roasted pecan halves (see p. 137)

Before untying watercress, trim bottom ½-inch off stems. Untie and remove any yellowed or bruised leaves. Rinse well under cold running water, then cut stems in 1-inch sections, leaving upper leaves intact. Arrange on each of 4 serving plates. Cut tips off sweet potato and peel off the skin. Cut in half lengthwise; cut each half across in ¼-inch slices. Arrange slices on the watercress, then add salt, lemon juice and oil as desired. Top with pecan halves.

Variations: Combine watercress with other salad greens for a milder salad; use A Simple Lemon Vinaigrette (see p. 20); add thin-sliced strips of Roasted Free-Range Chicken (see p. 104).

CABBAGE, CARROT AND CASHEW SALAD

Our word "salad" is believed to originate from the Latin "salata" meaning "salted." A traditional Japanese "pressed salad" is created by salting shredded vegetables, then pressing them with a weight while they sit for a while to let the salt draw water from them. The tender, glistening vegetables are then usually further seasoned.

This version uses less salt than traditional versions; rinse briefly after pressing if you want to reduce sodium further. The strongly-flavored oil adds a lot of flavor for little fat, making room for the cashews if you are watching your fat grams.

¼	head	(2 cups) cabbage, shredded thinly
1	medium	carrot, grated
¼	teaspoon	sea salt
1	tablespoon	cilantro, chopped
1	tablespoon	lemon juice
1	teaspoon	toasted sesame oil
	to taste	apple juice concentrate or other sweetener (optional)
¼	cup	raw cashews

Wash and prepare vegetables. Combine in a bowl with salt and stir to mix well; use hands to press into a mound; top vegetables with plate, then place a 2-3 pound weight (or water-filled bowl or jar) on the plate. Allow to stand for 20-30 minutes. Roast cashews on a pan in a toaster oven (or regular oven) at 325° for about 10 minutes or until lightly browned, shaking the pan once or twice to help brown evenly. Remove weight from plate; tilt bowl, holding plate in place to drain off any excess liquid (rinse vegetables and drain well if desired). Add remaining ingredients and stir to mix well. Flavor will develop more if allowed to rest for a while, but it's great right away, too!

Variation: For a creamier, conventional slaw-like texture, add ¼-½ cup Creamy Tofu Dressing (see p. 21).

4 servings

f you want to learn mathematics, you study books about math. If you want to learn about spirituality, you will study books on spirituality. If you think you can sit down and find joy without studying to gain clarified spiritual principles in your heart and mind, you may find yourself sitting in increasing boredom for a long, long time.

hy is spiritual reading a most necessary thing? All day long every day we are bombarded with data on visible and tangible things. All day every day our senses are impinged by visible, tangible things. All the years of our schooling were devoted to clarify and emphasize these visible and tangible things. How, then, shall we give importance and pride of place to what is beyond the visible and tangible unless we somehow, somewhere also ensure that these non-physical realities also impinge on us daily?

GROW YOUR OWN

Here's a way to bring the freshest produce possible to your table without nearly as much cost and fuel as required to produce what's trucked into your local market. Take any whole, unbroken and unsprayed seed, soak it in pure water, then let the process of life begin. For several days, the seed can grow without taking nutrients from the soil, feeding on the starch within itself. Miraculously, nutrients present only in trace amounts in the dried seed increase many times over. "Sprouts" contain good amounts of vitamins A, B, C and E, as well as high quality protein. During World War I, efforts to cure "scurvy" (vitamin C deficiency) proved sprouted beans more effective than lemons! Because sprouted seeds expand up to 20 times in volume, these are among the most economical of foods.

3	tablespoons	alfalfa seeds
1	cup	pure water

Place seeds in a wide-mouth glass 1-quart jar, add water. Soak seeds in a dark place for 6 hours. Cover jar with a piece of cheesecloth secured tightly with a strong piece of string or rubber band. Drain off soaking water, then rinse the seeds with fresh water and drain again. Set jar at a 45° angle away from direct sunlight, with open end down, to allow excess moisture to drain. Rinse the sprouts twice a day with fresh water, allowing them to drain thoroughly each time. When they are 1-2 inches long (4-5 days), place the jar in a sunnier location (indirect light is fine) for several hours to increase the production of chlorophyll and beta-carotenes, which will cause the leaves to become greener. When ready to harvest, place the sprouts in a bowl or sink full of cold water and stir the sprouts gently to loosen the hulls. Some will sink to the bottom. Skim off those that float to the surface. Lift the sprouts out of the water without disturbing the hulls below; drain well, then transfer to a clean glass jar or plastic bag. Refrigerate; use within 7-10 days.

Variation: Spicy Sprout Blend: replace 1 tablespoon of the alfalfa seeds with 1 tablespoon of radish or mustard seeds. Zing!

3½-4 cups

*A*sublime spiritual teacher once taught that "Death is absolutely safe." But so is life! There is no danger along our way, only optional delay. We are free to choose the speed with which we travel—free to choose, as it were, to repeat the seventh grade over and over, but living is always safe. It could be said that the reason this is so is the point of all meditation and spiritual striving.

*S*omeone wrote somewhere, somewhat cynically, "Reincarnation is for the ignorant." Whether or not you choose to believe in reincarnation, try to appreciate the point being made. It is well taken. We will continue to work at becoming fully conscious, one way or another, until we "get it right." The whole of the human race's deepest spiritual tradition from all over the earth tells us that what we are trying to "get right" is not obedience to a set of directives, but full awareness of the nature of the Reality that we share.

TOASTED SESAME AND ORANGE DRESSING

The special flavor of toasted sesame oil combined with the essence of orange makes this dressing special.

¼	cup	unrefined sesame oil or canola oil
¼	cup	toasted sesame oil
¼	cup	lemon juice
⅓	cup	orange juice
	zest of one	orange (organically-grown)
1	tablespoon	naturally-brewed soy sauce (or salt, to taste)

Combine all ingredients in a blender or glass jar; blend on high speed (or shake at your speed) to blend ingredients well. Allow flavors to blend for 5-10 minutes before serving, if possible.

a bit more than a cup

SIMPLE LEMON VINAIGRETTE

This is the dressing I enjoy most often. It is ready as quickly as you can squeeze a lemon and shake, shake, shake. Find a good, simple manual lemon juicer - one which strains the seeds and is easily cleaned. The sweetener is optional; if the lemon is sweet and the oil has a "fruity" flavor, it's really not needed. A classic vinaigrette uses 3-4 times as much oil, resulting in a milder flavor, but, of course, with a much higher fat content. This one is more tangy; add it sparingly to your simple salads to allow the delicate taste of the greens to speak to your body!

¼	cup	extra virgin olive oil
¼	cup	lemon juice or mild rice vinegar
1	teaspoon	light honey (optional)
		salt and/or pepper to taste

Combine all ingredients in a jar or dressing bottle. Close tightly and shake to blend well. Shake well again just before serving. Enjoy!

Variation: Add 1 teaspoon prepared mustard and 1 teaspoon each of your favorite fresh herbs (use ¼ teaspoon if dried herbs are used): try basil, thyme, oregano, marjoram and/or chervil. A bit of minced fresh garlic is great, too!

Note: If you have leftovers, ask the last person to use it to close the lid tightly!

about ½ cup

*N*ew insights seem dangerous and folly to those who limit their wisdom to repeating the familiar. They are like adults who remember their mother's childhood warning about not crossing a street without holding someone's hand, but never come to recognize that what she was really teaching was not about holding hands but about not being careless with one's life. Be patient with yourself if you are not yet comfortable with what are new insights to you. Be alert, too, not to criticize others who go about simply repeating old bromides. But do strive fearlessly not to let either their or your own strongly held and often loudly spoken familiar presuppositions cause you to slacken your own passion for full consciousness and a genuinely contemplative experience of your world.

CREAMY TOFU DRESSING OR SANDWICH SPREAD

Tofu originated in China over 2,000 years ago, and has nourished Asian peoples since with a very digestible form of high quality, inexpensive soy protein. Low in saturated fat and cholesterol, its popularity today is also due to its convenience and versatility. Various types of tofu and preparation methods offer a wide range of textures, and the subtle flavor allows this food to accept almost any seasoning well. For dips, dressings and puddings, "silken" type tofu is the best choice.

This simple dressing provides a great vehicle for experimentation with fresh herbs. Prepared without the water or additional seasoning, it is similar in texture and taste to mayonnaise. Add your favorite herbs and seasonings to either version, and savor the results on a simple salad.

1	(10.5-ounce package)	silken tofu, firm style, drained
3	tablespoons	lemon juice or brown rice vinegar
5	tablespoons	extra virgin olive or canola oil
3	tablespoons	miso, white or beige variety (or sea salt to taste)
¼ -⅓	cup	water, to thin for dressing consistency

For a sandwich spread, combine all ingredients but the water in a blender or food processor and puree until completely smooth. Add water if desired to thin to dressing consistency. Adjust seasoning to suit your taste.

Variation: Try adding 1 teaspoon of one of the following chopped herbs after pureeing in the blender; allow flavors to blend for an hour before deciding to add more: tarragon, thyme, oregano, parsley, savory, dill, basil, chervil, or chives.

Note: If using salt instead of miso, add 1-3 teaspoons of concentrated sweetener to taste.

*Y*ou may at times be tempted to criticize others for what you often do yourself. Without any doubt, everybody is on his or her own cutting edge and is acting from that most understandable drive common to us all, self-preservation. In their religious practices your brothers and sisters are undoubtedly trying to be safe and secure with God, howsoever they understand that term. Never question others' religious motives. Smile with compassionate humor for both yourself and them as you recall those times when, lacking clear consciousness, you, too, surrounded yourself with rules and rituals of guilt and fear to reassure yourself that your relationship with God was safe.

HERBED ORANGE OR APRICOT-MUSTARD DRESSING

This tangy dressing is also good as a marinade and basting sauce for grilled vegetables or chicken (see p. 55).

¼	cup	olive oil
⅓	cup	water
¼	cup	orange or apricot spread
¼	cup	stone ground mustard
½	teaspoon	sage, dried
½	teaspoon	oregano

Combine all ingredients in a tightly covered container; shake to blend well. Allow flavors to blend at least an hour before using.

about 1 cup

ROASTED GARLIC DRESSING

Use the soft and mellow paste of the garlic you've roasted (see An Ovenful of Simple Veggies, p. 44) to make this creamy vinaigrette.

3	tablespoons	roasted garlic paste (2-3 bulbs of roasted garlic, depending on size)
⅓	cup	lemon juice, fresh
3	tablespoons	extra virgin olive oil
¼	teaspoon	sea salt (optional)
½	teaspoon	oregano
¼	teaspoon	thyme, dry or 1 teaspoon fresh, minced

In a small bowl, use a whisk or fork to stir the lemon juice into the garlic paste a bit at a time to create a smooth texture. Add remaining ingredients, rubbing dry thyme, if used, between two fingers to release flavor; stir well. Transfer to a "shakeable" glass jar or other container. Allow flavors to mingle at least 10 minutes if possible before serving, or enjoy it right away, then again when taste is fully developed!

Variation: Combine all ingredients in a blender and blend until smooth.

almost ¾ cup

t will be an unfortunate person who will lightly turn away in disbelief from the data and experience of the world's most enlightened individuals for the sake of familiar doctrines and thought. This will be all the more unfortunate if the beliefs they cling to have, in fact, led not to universal love and well-being but to centuries of religious wars and bigotries and oppression. One might suggest to them: if your old ideas have not worked, why not try new ones? And if these so-called "new" ideas have the endorsement of centuries of the race's most peaceful and loving individuals, all the better!

Soups & Stews

I NOURISH MYSELF WITH NATURALLY-GROWN, MINIMALLY-PROCESSED FOODS, WHICH ARE IDEALLY SUITED TO SUPPORT LIFE.

Food (food) n. 1. any nourishing substance that is eaten or otherwise taken into the body to sustain life, provide energy, promote growth, etc.…

The natural, physical structure of each plant or animal is a result of a complex interaction of many different energies. Water, soil nutrients, sunlight, seasonal changes, human care…all cooperate with unseen forces to create each unique form of life. I can nourish myself with foods which are close to these natural forms, full of the vibrant forces of Life. I can select foods which have been nourished by naturally-healthy soil, tended by those who give back to it more than they take. As I provide for my own needs in this way, I support the health of the earth as well.

SOUPS AND STEWS

Hearty and warming or light and cooling, soups and stews prepared with loving care and nutrient-rich natural ingredients offer even more than potent, preventive and healing medicine: they taste good! Something magical happens when simmering liquid draws on the flavors of its companions, gently blending them with the love of the cook.

Begin with the highest-quality ingredients available. Unrefined foods grown naturally on healthy soil bring vitality to your broth. Save your vegetable trimmings (and leftover bones, if you eat meat, poultry or fish). Let them enrich a stock on a day when you're around the house for a while anyway, then freeze what you won't use soon. Even without a stock, delicious soups can be just minutes away when you have a variety of intentional leftovers on hand. Any cooked whole grain, bean or vegetable can provide the foundation of a simple soup or stew. Flavorful and healing herbs and spices allow for an endless number of simple and unusual combinations. Make a note of those you like most.

FROM THE HEART

1-2	cups	cooked grain, pasta or beans (see pp. 75 and 65)
1-2	cups	one or more fresh, frozen or pre-cooked vegetables, sliced or diced
	just enough	cool water or stock to cover
	a pinch	or dash of an herb or two (use 4-6 times as much fresh as you'd use dry)
	a bit	of fresh, bright color - scallions or parsley, shredded carrot, purple onion
one	gallon	loving kindness

Set aside any pre-cooked vegetables to add near end of cooking. Combine first five ingredients in non-reactive pot and bring to a simmer. Cook over low heat for 10-20 minutes, or until vegetables are tender; add any cooked veggies used with the colorful things; simmer another minute or so. Season to taste while you stir in the love. Share it.

Yield: As much as you want to make

THE RESOURCEFUL POT

The stockpot has long been valued as a way to conserve otherwise wasted flavor and nutrients of the harvest. Though a poultry or meat stock requires longer cooking than a vegetable stock, the preparation is essentially the same. Ingredients are covered with cold water and brought slowly to a boil, then simmered for as little as 1 hour for a vegetable stock and up to an 6 hours for meat-based stocks.

Next time you trim off the ends of an onion, carrot or celery stalk, or remove the bones from a roasted chicken or turkey, consider freezing them for a simple stock. Kombu, a dried sea vegetable rich in trace minerals, contains a natural flavor enhancer which works particularly well with shiitake mushrooms. Any vegetable can be useful, but be cautious with strongly-flavored members of the cabbage family, and avoid the use of outer leaves of vegetables which may have been sprayed with chemicals of any kind.

The liquid from canned beans is a fiber-rich alternative to some of the water.

2	cups	onion trimmings (or 1-2 whole onions)
	tops & ends	from one bunch of celery
½-1	cup	carrot trimmings
1-2	cups	parsley stems and/or sprigs, chopped coarsely
1	leaf	bay leaf
3-4	sprigs	fresh thyme (or ½-1 teaspoon dried)
1	(5-inch) stick	kombu
2	medium	shiitake mushrooms, dried
	bones of one	free-range chicken or turkey or 1-2 pounds natural meat bones (optional)
		water and/or bean broth

Remove any bruised or discolored parts of vegetables; wash well. Place all ingredients in a stockpot with enough cold water to cover by several inches. Bring slowly to a boil, then reduce heat and simmer, with bubbles barely breaking the surface, for 1 hour if vegetable stock, 3 hours for the poultry version, and 6 hours for the meat version. Strain the stock through a fine-mesh strainer or cheesecloth-lined colander; return to the pot and continue to simmer to reduce its volume by up to ½. If meat or poultry is used, cool as quickly as possible in a bowl surrounded by ice, or set the pot in a sinkful of cold water.

Refrigerate. When chilled, skim any fat off surface; refrigerate up to five days; freeze up to one year.

*C*onsider this. If a grammar school schedule calls for four recess periods every school day, and if four teachers each monitor one of the recesses, it is likely that the children will know four sets of rules for their play. The teachers' individual backgrounds and temperaments will cause them to differ as to how they seek to achieve their common goal of safety and fair recreation on the playground. Hopefully, by the time the children become adults they will recognize the single purpose in their former teachers' different styles and will no longer think of their efforts as having been arbitrary and whimsical, competitive and contradictory. Just so, we each have an opportunity in today's world of travel and shared insight to appreciate the plurality of style, but essential unity of purpose, in all of the world's religions.

SPICED BUTTERNUT SQUASH SOUP

East Indian spices and herbs add warming zest and interesting contrast to this richly-colored, sweet and nutritious soup. Cilantro, the leafy part of the coriander plant, has a flavor usually either appreciated greatly or not at all, so use it sparingly if you haven't tried it yet. Cooking changes the flavor; some may like it better stirred into the soup during the last few minutes of cooking.

Maybe God made green and orange look so good together because we need our beta-carotene.

1	tablespoon	ghee (see p. 70) or canola oil
1	teaspoon	whole black or brown mustard seeds
1	tablespoon	fresh ginger, minced
1	medium	yellow or white onion, finely-diced or chopped
2	or more cups	water or stock
3	cups	baked butternut or buttercup squash, skin removed
	to taste	sea salt
	to taste	lemon juice
		dairy or soy yogurt or sour cream (optional)
2-4	tablespoons	chopped fresh cilantro or parsley

Heat ghee or oil in a large saucepan or skillet over medium heat. Add mustard seeds and sauté for a few seconds, or until they begin to crackle and pop. Add ginger, sauté for 15 seconds; add onion, stir well and sauté until it begins to brown, stirring occasionally. While onion is cooking, combine squash and 2 cups of water or stock in a blender or food processor. Puree until smooth, adding enough liquid to get a thick soup consistency. Add squash puree to saucepan or skillet, stir well, add salt to taste and allow to simmer for 5-10 minutes. Stir in lemon juice to taste. Serve each bowl of soup garnished with yogurt and chopped fresh cilantro.

7 cups

Variation: Substitute plain, non-fat yogurt for one or more cups of the water or stock for a tangier taste; adjust liquid and seasonings to suit yourself.

MEDITERRANEAN LENTIL SOUP

The combination of ground coriander and cumin offers a special flavor to this soup. Herbalists say these seeds have "carminative" properties, referring to the ability to prevent or relieve intestinal gas. Both have been used for thousands of years with lentils, the protein-rich, lens-shaped legume (yes, that's where the word lens came from), which was one of the first crops ever cultivated. Whatever they do, the taste is good. Carry on the tradition, and share it with a friend. Freeze the extra for busier days.

1	cup	dry green or brown lentils
5	cups	water or stock
1		bay leaf
2	medium	carrots, cut in half lengthwise, then sliced in ¼-inch half-moons
1	stalk	celery, sliced ¼-inch thick
1	bunch	scallions, trimmed, sliced ¼-inch thick, green tops separated from white part
1	teaspoon	coriander, ground
2	teaspoons	cumin, ground
½	teaspoon	thyme, dried (or 1 tablespoon fresh)
½	teaspoon	freshly-ground black pepper
	to taste	sea salt or naturally-brewed soy sauce
	to taste	lemon juice

Prepare lentils as described in The Basic Pot of Beans, p. 65, adding bay leaf during last hour of cooking, or combine dry lentils, water and bay leaf in a large saucepan over high heat; bring to a boil; reduce heat to low and simmer until lentils are tender, about 45 minutes. Add vegetables (reserving green part of scallions), coriander, cumin and thyme; simmer until vegetables are tender, 20-30 minutes. Add extra water or stock as needed for desired consistency; add salt or soy sauce to taste 10 minutes before end of cooking, and scallion greens at the end. Stir well, remove from heat, add lemon juice to taste and serve. Garnish with grated carrot or yogurt.

6-8 servings

*P*lurality of religions is like plurality in the earth's languages. It is good to be grateful for the finesse of your native tongue that gives you the ability to share your feelings and thoughts with others, but in no way is it a betrayal of this gratitude if you go on to learn other languages. On the contrary, coming to appreciate the unique subtleties of other languages helps you return to your native tongue with new appreciation of its own special genius. It is exactly the same regarding humankind's many varieties of religion and spirituality. They all enrich each other.

*T*o appreciate all the religious efforts made by our race does not mean we may no longer be especially loyal to our own familiar tradition. It does, however, require two attitudes in us: that we now be willing to look more critically into our own beliefs and that we leave all competitiveness and bigotry behind.

FRESH CORN CHOWDER

Mellow and comforting. If you want to have extra fun, put the roasted pepper garnish in a pastry bag and decorate each bowl of soup with a dancing heart or two.

2	ears	fresh corn on the cob
2	cups	water or stock
1	small	bay leaf
1	small	onion, finely chopped
8	ounces	red potato, (peeled if desired) and cubed ½-inch
1	stalk	celery, halved lengthwise, then sliced thinly
2	tablespoons	canola oil
3	tablespoons	unbleached white flour
1	cup	skim milk, soy or almond milk
	to taste	sea salt and pepper
¼	cup	Roasted Red Pepper Garnish (see next page)
2	tablespoons	chopped fresh parsley

Shave corn kernels off the cob using a sharp knife; set corn aside. Measure water or stock into a stockpot; add corn cobs and bay leaves; bring to a boil; reduce heat to low and cover; simmer 15 minutes. Meanwhile, prepare onion, potato and celery. Remove cobs and bay leaves from stock; add potato, onion and celery, bring back to a boil, reduce heat to low and simmer until potato is almost tender, about 10 minutes. Add corn and simmer another 10 minutes. While corn simmers, make the roux: measure oil and flour into a small skillet or saucepan; stir well and bring to a simmer over medium-low heat. Simmer 3 minutes, stirring occasionally. Stir roux into simmering soup; continue to stir until broth thickens. Add milk. Puree half of soup in a blender to create a thicker, creamier texture. Add salt and pepper to taste; simmer 3-5 more minutes. Garnish with swirls or hearts of Roasted Red Pepper Garnish; sprinkle parsley on last.

Quick Variation: Substitute 10 ounces frozen corn for fresh; omit simmering cobs in the stock.

4 servings

A person who is truly free will appreciate the wisdom of a modern Sufi master who, when asked what church he belonged to, replied simply, "I belong to no church; they all belong to me."

*T*he Golden Rule urging us to love one another has been stated in every religious culture in the world with only the most superficial differences of grammar and usage. The hearts and minds of human beings everywhere have obviously all been finding essentially the same Wisdom throughout the ages. This race-wide effort and its identical core conclusions were not yet recognized in the ancient Near East or in medieval Europe where the majority of the western world's religious presuppositions were formed. But they *are* recognized today! We only impoverish ourselves if we live on as though the earth has not grown smaller and our awareness larger.

ROASTED RED PEPPER GARNISH

You can roast and peel the peppers yourself, but the bottled variety are fairly good. The striking salmon-red hue makes for a nice contrast on any light-colored vegetable soup. See recipes for Roasted Pepper Vinaigrette (see p. 16) and Broccoli Bliss (see p. 111) for other uses for this simple blend.

1	(7-ounce)	bottle red pepper, roasted
1	teaspoon	fresh thyme (or ¼ teaspoon dried)
1	clove	garlic, fresh
1-2	tablespoons	olive oil, extra virgin
	to taste	sea salt

Drain peppers; press to drain as much liquid as possible. Strip thyme leaves from stem; peel garlic. Combine drained peppers with thyme, garlic and oil and puree in a blender or food processor until smooth. Add salt to taste; puree to blend. Allow flavors to blend for 30 minutes before using, if possible, especially if using dried thyme.

½-⅔ **cup**

*T*t is too simple to reduce God's Universe to a juridical system, to just a matter of obeying divine decrees. That was the guidance given our race in its earliest childhood, much as parents surround young children with do's and don'ts. Parents always, however, await the day when their offspring will graduate to something more insightful. We have a journey to make, a journey into conscious awareness of our eternal Origin, into deep awareness of who and what we Are. Our journey is not to acquire what we already have, but to realize it.

A concerned old farewell stated "Keep the faith!" The intention was good, but the statement is unfortunate, even cruel. It implies that if we maintain assent with our minds to a certain set of concepts and dictates, we will find happiness. "*Be* the faith" says it better. But we must be careful what we mean by the word *faith*.

SOUP FOR A HAPPY HEART
(THREE-MUSHROOM, BARLEY AND LEEK)

Garlic, shiitake mushrooms and barley each benefit the cardiovascular system in their own way.

Make this soup with a friend to enhance the effect.

2	tablespoons	olive oil or ghee (see p. 70)
1-2	tablespoons	fresh garlic, minced
2	medium	leeks
3-4	ounces	(2 cups each) fresh shiitake, oyster and brown or button mushrooms
¼	teaspoon	thyme
¼	teaspoon	sea salt
3	cups	water or stock
2	cups	well-cooked barley (see p. 73)
2	tablespoons	naturally-brewed soy sauce, low sodium type
	to taste	freshly-ground black pepper
	for garnish	chopped fresh chervil or parsley

Cut off root end of leeks, remove any wilted or bruised outer leaves and tips, then cut off (and save for a stock!) the green leaves 2 inches above the white part. Slice in half lengthwise and thoroughly rinse under cold running water to remove any sand or dirt; slice thinly in half-moon shapes. Trim tough stems off shiitake mushrooms and dried or brown ends from others. Wipe clean with a damp cloth or mushroom brush. Slice ¼-inch thick.

Heat oil or ghee in a large saucepan; add garlic and sauté 10 seconds. Add leeks, mushrooms, thyme and salt; stir well and sauté until vegetables are wilted and volume is reduced by half. Add water or stock and barley. Bring to a simmer over high heat, reduce heat to low and simmer for 15-20 minutes.

Add soy sauce for last 5 minutes of cooking. Serve warm with black pepper and chopped fresh herbs.

Variation: If you have no barley, substitute ⅔ cup uncooked rolled oats and use 1½ cups extra liquid.

6-8 servings

*T*he challenge for you as a person at this place in human evolution is no longer that you cling tenaciously to a set of given doctrines, but that you see and live ever more completely a higher vision of Life. That is "faith" in its fullest meaning. You are invited today to live ever more consciously and with an ever higher, deeper and broader experience of the Universe. Almost 6,000 years of the now-collated spiritual wisdom of our race suggests that we are each called to realize the "Oneness with the Father" that Jesus spoke of and that every spiritual master before him and since has spoken of. And it is not that we are asked merely to assent to this with our minds: it must be felt, sensed, experienced. Our human family has now tried all other paths to peace and bliss and found them wanting.

RED BEAN AND YELLOW SQUASH CHILI

Traditional chili is a great example of using small amounts of "complete" animal protein to boost the usability of bean protein, which is deficient in one of the essential amino acids we need to be able to utilize it efficiently. In the meatless version, the amino acid strengths and deficiencies of grain and bean protein complement each other, resulting in "complete" vegetable protein. The squash adds nice color and helps create a complete meal. The size of this batch suggests either freezing some for future quick meals or inviting some friends to share!

2	tablespoons	vegetable oil
1	pound	ground turkey, natural beef or venison (optional)
1	large	onion, diced
1	medium	bell pepper, core and seeds removed, diced
28	ounces	whole, peeled tomatoes, canned, preferrably organically-grown
1	(16 ounce)	can tomato puree
3	cups	(2 16-ounce cans) cooked kidney beans, with liquid
1	cup	cracked wheat (or 1½ cups textured vegetable protein), if you're making a meatless version
¼	cup	chili powder
2	teaspoons	oregano, dried
2	tablespoons	cumin, ground
3	cups	yellow squash, trimmed and cut in 1-inch chunks
2-4	tablespoons	naturally-brewed soy sauce to taste
1	teaspoon	black pepper, ground
½	cup	purple onion or scallions, chopped, for garnish

Heat oil in a large pot over medium-high heat. Add turkey or meat, if used, with onion and bell pepper; sauté until meat has browned. Add next seven ingredients; stir well. Raise heat and bring just to a boil. Reduce heat to low; cover; simmer for 20 minutes, stirring occasionally. Add squash; raise heat to bring back to a simmer; continue to cook until squash is tender, about 15 - 20 minutes. Season to taste.

about 12 cups

The word *mystics* must be understood accurately. It does not mean, and must not be read as meaning, someone given to weirdness and not to real life. The word comes from a Greek verb meaning "to initiate." In Greek a *mystikos* is one who has been initiated into the inner truths and meaning of a given subject. A trained and experienced physicist, for example, is technically a mystic. He knows the inside knowledge and practice of physics. As used in spiritual contexts, a religious mystic is simply someone who has seen, has experienced, the inner side of religion and so, by definition, of Ultimate Reality. Contrary to a too-frequent connotation attached to the word in the West, *mystic* carries no meaning whatsoever of strangeness or lack of contact with reality. Quite the contrary!

QUICK VEGETABLE SAMBAAR (EAST INDIAN BEAN AND VEGETABLE CURRY)

Jazz up some canned soup for something different when you're in a hurry.

2	tablespoons	vegetable oil or clarified butter
1-2	tablespoons	minced fresh ginger
1	tablespoon	whole cumin seed
1	tablespoon	whole brown mustard seed
1	tablespoon	mild or hot curry powder, sambaar powder or garam masala
½	cup	diced onion
1	tablespoon	garlic, minced
1	16-ounce	can lentil soup
1	16-ounce	can split pea soup
10	ounces	frozen mixed vegetables or frozen spinach
		-or-
2	cups	leftover steamed vegetables
½	cup	fresh cilantro, chopped (¼ cup for cooking, ¼ cup for garnish)
½	teaspoon	salt, or to taste
1	medium	tomato, diced ½-inch
¼	cup	sliced, toasted almonds

Heat oil or butter in a large skillet; add ginger and sauté for about 30 seconds; add cumin and mustard seed and sauté until mustard seeds begin to pop, about 15 - 30 seconds. Add curry or sambaar powder or garam masla and stir for 10 seconds. Add onion and sauté until almost translucent.

If needed, add a few tablespoons of water to prevent sticking. Add garlic with soup, vegetables and half of the cilantro. Bring just to a boil; reduce heat to low and simmer until vegetables are very tender, about 5 - 10 minutes. Add salt to taste. Ladle over brown or basmati rice or serve as is for a one-dish meal or soup. Garnish with tomato, almonds and remaining cilantro.

Variation: For a spicier taste, add minced, fresh jalapeño or sliced green chili peppers with the curry or sambaar powder, but **don't breathe the fumes.** *Or add cayenne pepper to taste at the end.*

serves 4 - 6

F or centuries the pope was taken to important functions on a chair eight men carried on their shoulders. This portable throne was known as his *sedia gestatoria*, his "carrying chair." It was seen in a previous day as a thing of high office and great dignity. Appreciate your body, if you will, as your *sedia gestatoria* for your time on this earth. Far more than any piece of gilt furniture, it is a reality and sign of great dignity. There is no suggestion here that you parade about with solemnity and pomp, but there is the reminder to move about consciously aware that you deserve, and by Nature are, a person of great dignity. Carry your dignity lightheartedly, but consciously carry it.

CARIBBEAN BLACK BEAN AND VEGETABLE SOUP

More people tell me they like black beans than any other. Maybe it has something to do with the Mexican or Caribbean seasonings commonly used. I favor this soup with chunks of vegetables and some whole beans, rather than pureed. During one cooking class, a group of inventive students stirred the vegetables intended for garnish into their batch of soup - with marvelous results! Here is their version:

5	cups	cooked black beans with cooking liquid (about 2 cups dry beans)
1	large	bay leaf
2	tablespoons	extra virgin olive oil
1	large	onion, diced
1	each	medium green and gold bell pepper, diced
¼	teaspoon	sea salt
2	tablespoons	cumin, ground
1	tablespoon	chili powder
2	teaspoons	oregano, dry
⅛-¼	teaspoon	cayenne pepper
2-4	tablespoons	naturally-brewed soy sauce, to taste
¼	cup	lime juice
2	medium	vine-ripened tomatoes, diced
½	cup	purple onion, thinly sliced
		plain yogurt or sour cream
		paprika or chopped parsley

Cook beans as described in The Basic Pot of Beans (see p. 65) adding bay leaf for last hour of cooking. Heat oil in a large skillet or stockpot over medium heat; add onion, peppers and salt; sauté for 2-3 minutes, or until onion is translucent. Add seasonings, soy sauce, lime juice and beans to vegetables; bring to a boil; reduce heat and simmer 15-30 minutes. Just before serving, stir tomato and onion into the hot soup. Serve immediately, garnished with dollops of yogurt or sour cream and paprika or parsley.

Variation: Substitute 3 (16-ounce) cans cooked blackened beans for home-cooked taste.

8 (1-cup) servings

*Y*our body is not the enemy of your soul, as various religions have taught. Quite the contrary; it is your inseparable companion, part of your very self. How could it be in any degree your enemy? Think of your complete body as you think of your right hand. You willingly cleanse, nourish and groom your hand. You give it direction with your higher faculties so that it does not reach into another's purse or hit anyone. But you never treat it badly or consider it to be your enemy. Maltreating or malnourishing the body, by design or default—even denying it its gentle comforts and pleasures—comes from an erroneous understanding of its place in the Universe, in *your* Universe.

CALYPSO SOUP

An heirloom variety Spanish bean with a wonderful blend of spices to lighten your heart.

2	tablespoons	olive oil
1	teaspoon	fennel seeds, whole
1	large	onion, diced
1	medium	gold pepper
1	medium	carrot
1	cup	cabbage, diced
¼	teaspoon	sea salt
4	medium	ripe tomatoes, peeled and chopped, with liquid (to peel, see note below)
2	cups	cooked calypso beans, with liquid (may substitute red beans)
1	cup	water or stock
1	large	bay leaf
1	tablespoon	paprika
2	teaspoons	basil
¼	teaspoon	cinnamon, ground
¾	teaspoon	allspice
½	teaspoon	ground ginger
⅛	teaspoon	freshly grated nutmeg
		cayenne or black pepper, to taste

Heat oil in a large saucepan over medium heat. Add fennel seeds and cook for 20 seconds, stirring continuously. Add onion, bell pepper, carrot and cabbage with salt; sauté until onion and cabbage are wilted, stirring occasionally. Add remaining ingredients except pepper; bring just to a boil; reduce heat and simmer for 20-30 minutes, covered. Add pepper to taste.

Quick Variation: Replace fresh tomatoes with 1 (28-ounce) can peeled tomatoes.

Note: To peel fresh tomatoes, immerse in boiling water for 30-60 seconds, then transfer to a bowl of cold water. The peel should easily rinse off after scoring with a knife, if necessary.

6-8 servings

HEARTY JAPANESE RED BEAN STEW WITH WINTER SQUASH

Azuki beans, popular in Japan for over 1,500 years, are considered by folk medicine to be helpful for kidney problems. These, small, deep red, oblong beans do not require soaking. I still prefer to prepare them as described in The Basic Pot of Beans (see p. 65), which results in a rich gravy if you let them cook long enough. This warming, soothing stew goes right to the core of your being. The combination of sweetness, ginger, garlic and onion is magical. Try it in improvised soups and side dishes.

4	cups	cooked azuki beans with "gravy" (or 1 ½ cups dry and 4½ cups water)
2	tablespoons	canola oil
1-2	tablespoons	fresh ginger, peeled and minced
1	medium	onion, diced about the size of a cooked bean
2-3	cups	butternut squash peeled and diced (½-inch chunks) or
1-2	each	carrot and parsnip, trimmed and peeled if desired, diced
½	cup	water
¼	teaspoon	sea salt
1	tablespoon	fresh garlic, minced
2	tablespoons	miso, deep red or brown variety or soy sauce, or salt, to taste
		chopped parsley for garnish

If using dry beans, sort to remove rocks or debris, rinse briefly, then bring to a boil in water; reduce heat and simmer until very tender, stirring occasionally to help gravy develop. Cut root vegetables, if used, lengthwise in quarters, then in ¼-inch slices. Heat oil in a large saucepan over medium heat. Add ginger and onion; sauté until onion is translucent, about 2 minutes. Add squash or root vegetables and salt; sauté, stirring occasionally for 2-3 minutes. Add ½ cup of water and bring liquid to a boil; reduce heat to medium-low, add garlic, cover and simmer until vegetables are tender but not mushy, about 10 minutes. Add extra liquid if needed to avoid sticking. In a small bowl, dissolve the miso in ¼ cup of water, stirring well until smooth. Add beans and miso mixture to vegetables; stir well and simmer at least 15 minutes to allow flavors to blend. Add more water as needed for desired consistency; adjust seasoning to taste.

Quick Variation: Use canned beans, simmering if needed to develop gravy. Grate carrot and parsnip to save time.

4-6 servings; freezes well.

*Y*ou will simply be unaware, not guilty, if you go about envying others for their beauty or talents, or if you despise yourself or others for apparent limitations. One day you will come to make no judgments in these matters, but for now, if you must judge at all, judge what is *meta physical*, beyond the physical. There you will find everyone is equally noble and Divine—including yourself and absolutely every other person. You will spring free of idolatry for the *symbols* of Wholeness in so far as you realize you and everyone else already possess that Wholeness.

CHICKEN OR TOFU IN CLEAR BROTH WITH CUMIN, RED ONION, CILANTRO

Clear broth allows a few simple colors and shapes to be arranged in a feast for the eye as well as the belly.

1	teaspoon	whole cumin seeds
4½	cups	water or stock (see p. 26)
1	(6-8 ounce)	breast of free-range chicken (or 6 ounces tofu, drained)
1-2	teaspoons	juice of fresh ginger, squeezed from freshly grated ginger root
	to taste	sea salt
¼	medium	purple onion, thinly sliced
16-20	leaves	fresh cilantro, with stems removed
4	slices	lemon or lime for garnish

Roast cumin seeds in a dry saucepan over medium heat for 1-2 minutes; do not brown. Add water, bring to a boil, reduce heat to low and simmer for 5 minutes. Cut chicken or tofu into ½-inch cubes (partially freeze the chicken to make cutting easier). Add chicken or tofu to broth, bring just to a boil, reduce heat to low and simmer about 5 minutes. Add ginger juice, then salt to taste. Remove chicken from broth with a slotted spoon and transfer to 4 serving bowls. Arrange onion and cilantro leaves on top of chicken in each bowl. Stir broth, then pour an equal amount over each serving. Garnish with lemon slices.

Variation: Substitute 1-2 cups cooked chicken or turkey for the chicken breast.

4 servings

In the secret sanctuary of your innermost judgments, what is it that you think most validates or invalidates you and others? Bodily endowments? Academic degrees? Personality? Professional or social standing? You can reason with yourself all day every day about the unsuitableness of comparing yourself with others, but know that reasoning alone will never deliver you from this insidious habit. Why not turn the tables and use this silliness for your spiritual growth? Rather than criticize yourself, tell yourself—for it is a truth—that you have an inborn right to have all good things. *Earthly endowments are but intimations of the memory deep within your Spirit of its true Nature.* Remember this and you will rapidly come to feel validated and worthwhile beyond your wildest dreaming.

CURRIED GARBANZO AND MUSTARD GREEN SOUP

This dish was inspired by the "dals" of India which are sometimes cooked with greens. The creamy texture needed for this soup requires well-cooked beans and their own "gravy" (see p. 65). If you must use canned beans, try pureeing half of them in the blender before adding to the soup.

2	tablespoons	canola oil
1	tablespoon	whole cumin seeds
1	tablespoon	ginger, fresh, minced
1	small	onion, chopped
¼	teaspoon	sea salt
2	tablespoons	garlic, minced
2	cups	well-cooked garbanzo beans, with "gravy"
1	cup	cooked mustard greens (see p. 49), chopped
		-or-
10	ounces	frozen mustard greens, chopped, thawed and drained
2	cups	water or stock
¼	teaspoon	turmeric
		sea salt or lemon juice to taste
1	large	ripe tomato, diced
2	tablespoons	chopped cilantro or parsley

Heat oil in a saucepan over medium heat. Add cumin; sauté for 30 seconds; add ginger and sauté 30 seconds; add onion and salt, stir well; sauté until onions are translucent. Add garlic, beans, greens and water or stock. Bring to a boil; reduce heat to low and cover; simmer for 10 minutes or until greens are very tender. Remove from heat; season to taste. Garnish with tomatoes and cilantro.

4-6 servings

Image a great forest in which many varieties of trees grow side by side. There are stately cedars of regal dignity, soaring redwoods ready to touch the clouds, symmetrically perfect firs. But there are also lowly salal bushes, creeping ivies and ferns that seldom see the sun. Individual specimens in every species are twisted, fallen, torn and trampled. Some forest plants will never draw attention by their beauty, some never be "perfectly" shaped—if we define perfection by geometry and proportion of line. A thoughtful person will recognize that if every tree and bush were identically matched in height and shape, the forest would be artificial and boring. The human race is like a forest. Individual value and the beauty of the whole are not defined by superficial rules of appearance. Whatever our individual statures and shapes, we all together—and equally—make up the beauty of our race.

WAKAME-MISO SOUP

A simple vegetable soup does wonders on days when I feel the onset of a cold or the flu. Not sure why, but these symptoms have often disappeared completely after a few simple meals of a simple soup, along with plenty of rest and fluids. Wakame, a sea vegetable sold in dried form in Asian and natural foods markets, offers an abundance of trace minerals and calcium. Miso, another traditional Japanese food, is a naturally-fermented soybean paste which offers a rich, savory flavor along with digestion-enhancing enzymes, lactobacillus and other healthful microorganisms. Both these foods have traditionally been credited with the ability to maintain health and resist disease; modern studies as well have documented the effects of substances in each which help to bind with and neutralize excessive levels of radioactive elements, heavy metals and other environmental toxins in the human body. Whether or not you use these ancient foods, this soup has a balancing, calming effect. (See more about miso, p. 125).

1	tablespoon	fresh ginger, peeled and minced (optional)
1	medium	onion, sliced thinly
1	medium	carrot, halved lengthwise and sliced ¼-inch diagonally
2	cups	savoy or green cabbage, diced 1-inch square
5	cups	cold water or stock
6	(4-inch)	pieces wakame sea vegetable (optional)
1	cup	water
2-3	tablespoons	miso, deep red or brown variety (optional) or sea salt to taste

Soak wakame in 1 cup water in a small bowl until rehydrated, about 5-10 minutes. In a large saucepan, layer onion, carrot and cabbage in order given. Add water or stock; bring to a boil. Remove wakame from water, drain well and slice into bite-sized pieces. Add to soup. Also add soaking liquid, pouring carefully from bowl, allowing any sand to remain in bowl. When liquid boils, reduce heat to low and simmer until vegetables are tender, about 15-20 minutes. Use the small bowl to dissolve miso in ¼ cup of the warm broth, stirring until smooth. Add to the soup about 5 minutes before removing from heat. Do not boil after adding the miso.

about 8 cups

Once again, to press a most important point, think of the world as filled with millions of sacred sanctuaries. Some shine with marble and gold leaf as did the Taj Mahal the day it was completed. Some astound by the spaciousness of their proportions, as does St. Peter's in Rome. Some soar in intricate majesty like the cathedral at Chartres. Still others draw us by their mysterious past and haunting location, like those in the jungles of the Asian subcontinent. But many in every category are long since dusty, dilapidated and crumbling. And yet, by definition, they each remain sacred and worthy of reverence. So it is with the human race. Every individual, *including yourself and each of your neighbors,* is sacred and equally worthy of respect and reverence.

GAZPACHO SOUP WITH FRESH CORN AND CILANTRO

This cooling, nourishing blend is best when made with fresh, vine-ripened tomatoes, but the kind in the can will suffice in a pinch.

2	cups	tomato juice
¼	cup	red wine vinegar
2	tablespoons	extra virgin olive oil
2	large	ripe tomatoes, coarsely chopped, with juice
1	medium	cucumber, peeled if waxed, coarsely chopped
¼	small	purple onion, coarsely chopped
½	medium	bell pepper, coarsely chopped
2	cups	fresh corn, cut from 2 ears of cooked sweet yellow corn
¼	cup	parsley leaves
¼	cup	cilantro leaves
2	teaspoons	cumin, ground
¼	teaspoon	cayenne pepper, ground
	to taste	salt and/or freshly ground black pepper

Combine tomato juice, vinegar and olive oil with juice from chopped tomatoes; stir well to blend. Combine other vegetables in a mixing bowl; stir to blend. Puree vegetables (until chunky, not completely smooth) in small batches in a blender, using liquid ingredients as needed to help the blender do its job. Transfer each batch to a mixing bowl; add cumin and cayenne pepper; stir well to blend. Allow to rest for 2 - 4 hours before adjusting seasoning with salt and pepper to taste. Serve chilled.

Quick Variation: Substitute 16 ounces lightly steam frozen corn for fresh corn.

about 7 cups

*I*f you wish to experience the unfathomable peace and joy that comes with true enlightenment, you must determine once and for all that you will not be frightened by new insights. Far from harming you, "the truth will set you free!" Have you, for example, always been taught that God is separate from you and from the rest of creation? Most have, and traditional religious leaders in the West have always been outraged when mystics have suggested anything different — that, for instance, the Source Being individuates as ourSelves. That we are identified with the Divine Being is clearly stated in most of the world's sacred literature — including the Bible! People can realize that everyone is actually an outpressing of the Divine Life, after all, the rules and rulers of religious organizations would become significantly less important!

Enjoyable Vegetables

I ENHANCE MY HEALTH AND THAT OF THE EARTH WHEN I CHOOSE
FROM AS DIVERSE A VARIETY OF NATURAL FOODS AS POSSIBLE.

As natural ecosystems seek diversity to ensure stability, survival and
balance, so can I. Choosing from the full range of nourishment
available, I open to the abundant Life energy of these gifts of the earth.
Each natural food has a unique effect on my body, mind and spirit, and
I benefit most from consuming as many different types as possible. I
can gradually add unfamiliar foods to my diet, increasing the variety
of tastes, textures and colors I receive, reducing my need for the
extremes. I can learn about and harvest the native, wild edibles of my
area, for their energies are potent and strengthening. As I nourish
myself in this way, I support the health of the natural environment, for
the vitality of earth's soil, plants and animals, the quality of air and
water, all are improved when diversity is *allowed*!

ENJOYABLE VEGETABLES

Offering an incredible range of textures, tastes and nutrients, these potent gifts add never-ending interest to a diet of simple foods, providing nutrients and fiber which offer vital support to our health and protection from natural and modern imbalances. Ancient healers would not be surprised to learn that consumption of certain types of vegetables is related to reduced incidence of some cancers.

Included in this chapter are recipes for legumes and tubers. Both fit the dictionary definition, but each of these types of food are in their own special category. Heavier and more building in nature, they each combine well with other vegetables. In meal planning, tubers like potato, sweet potato or Jerusalem Artichoke usually take the place of a whole grain. Beans provide high quality protein, and serve as a solid foundation for meals which look to traditional ethnic cuisines of the world for inspiration.

Leaves, stems, bulbs and roots, flowering parts and fruits (like squash) - all offer gifts of uniqueness and balance. But of the 20,000 edible plants known, and the 3,000 species used for food throughout history, only 20 crops make up about 90 percent of the world's food supply today. Dependence upon such a limited resource base is not a wise use of what we've been given, nutritionally or ecologically.

Gladly, today's markets offer an increasing number of vegetables little known a decade ago. In addition, virtually every locale offers naturally-occurring edible wild plants of amazing diversity and nutritional potency, if they are permitted to grow. Used even occasionally to supplement market produce, they can add interest to meals and help deepen our relationship with nature.

To prepare vegetables well, prepare them simply.

THE SWEET AND SIMPLE ONES

> **2 carrots, organically-grown if possible**
>   **water for steaming**

Wash carrots, then slice diagonally into ¼-inch slices. Place in a steamer basket over boiling water and steam until tender. Eat simply, with gratitude. Notice how it feels.

Yield: Appreciation for a simple gift, one you may always remember.

There is a popular saying that "Whatever feels good is either fattening or sinful." Cute, perhaps, but indicative of a deep distrust and subtle cynicism. Move beyond such remarks quickly and realize that you have been endowed with an appetite for pleasurable experiences along with a resourceful mind that can fill that appetite. This combination of gifts is not to frustrate or try you, but to challenge your individual creativity. Your Nature does not ask you to deny your desires, but to discriminate in your selection of their fulfillment. Your life is an outpouring of Infinite Existence and has no room for snide and negative expressions of hopelessness and self-pity.

AN OVENFUL OF SIMPLE VEGGIES

Most of our meals on busy days are built around ingredients we've prepared ahead and stored in the refrigerator or freezer. One key to the success of this system is to prepare basic ingredients in very simple ways so they may be later used with versatility, depending on our needs or whims. Preparing it simply also allows us to experience food in its simplest form the first time around, while keeping prep time to a minimum. For example, after a few minutes of prep on a weekend morning, I can go on about my chores. Less than an hour later, I've got simple squash to eat with my eggs or scrambled tofu, and leftovers to use in Sweet Squash Spread for a snack the next day. Be sure to label and date your extras, so you'll know what you have. The quantities used depend on the size of your household.

1-2	winter squash
2-4	sweet potatoes or yams
2-4	baking potatoes and/or
8-10	new potatoes
1-3	whole onions
1-3	whole bulbs of garlic
	canola or extra virgin olive oil

Preheat oven to 400°. Rinse squash and scrub potatoes well; remove any eyes or green spots from potatoes and poke each several times with a fork. Break any stems off squash, cut in half and use a spoon to scrape out the seeds and stringy pulp. Cut off the top of each bulb of garlic to expose a bit of the cloves. Don't cut the root end or peel. Place all ingredients on one or two lightly oiled cookie sheets, with cut side of squash face down. Brush the garlic with oil, allowing some to soak into the cloves; oil potatoes if desired. Bake for 40-60 minutes, checking small potatoes after 30 minutes to remove when tender. Squash and potatoes are done when they yield easily to an inserted fork; garlic when soft.

Squash for Tangy Stuffed Squash (see p. 95), or Butternut Squash Butter, (see p. 90), sweet potatoes for use with Easy Cinnamon-Orange Sauce, (see p. 59), potatoes for Fragrant Potato & Broccoli Skillet Hash (see p. 56), onions for use on a simple salad, garlic for use in Roasted Garlic Dressing (see p. 22).

In so far as you begin truly to respect your body and life, you begin to take loving care of them. In so far as you recognize the identical Reality in every other person and thing, you begin to be equally concerned for all. Make one exception in your thinking and you deny yourself the purity of vision which alone permits unconstrained dancing in your heart.

LATE SUMMER WISDOM

I was 20 years old at college when an elderly neighbor handed me the first yellow squash I'd ever seen, straight from her garden. One of those crook-necked kind, it was small and dense, not like the tough-skinned, spongy ones they leave on the vine too long. Being in the habit of canned and frozen, I didn't quite know what to do with it. Cut it in slices, she said, and brown each side in a skillet with some butter. I tried it that afternoon, and knew right then I would learn more about these things.

The broiler method allows you to cook a larger amount all at once; use a skillet if you're cooking for one or two. Add some other seasonings or use olive oil if you like, but try it her way first.

2-3	small	yellow squash, not picked too long ago
1-2	tablespoons	melted butter or ghee (see p. 70)

Preheat oven broiler. Wash squash; trim off stems and tips; slice squash into ¼-inch rounds.

Lightly brush a cookie sheet with a small amount of the melted butter. Arrange squash on pan in one layer. Use remaining butter to brush the top of each slice. Broil until lightly browned, about 3-5 minutes on each side, turning once. Serve 'em hot. They happen to go great with brown rice and Roasted Sesame Condiment.

The flavor is noticeably better when the squash is in season and locally-grown with love.

2-4 servings

You will experience a subtle joy from properly caring for your body. This joy is not unlike the one you get from high spiritual insights. To deliberately select, prepare and consume foods you have come to understand to be good for your body and in no way harmful begets a unique sort of inner satisfaction. So is the feeling you get from learning to take unrushed time for a pleasurable bath or for a book that has no practical purpose other than your enjoyment. The body is not a mechanical device like a lawnmower that can be driven without love. It deserves and will reward you in many ways for the loving care you give it.

WINTER VEGETABLE BRAISE

I think of "winter vegetables" as those which were more commonly con-
sumed in cold weather before modern processing methods made possible the
variety we now see year-round. Braising refers to the process of sautéing
food in oil, then simmering slowly in very little liquid, either in the oven or a
skillet. Adding some salt to vegetables while sautéing draws out some of the
natural liquid, and, especially in the case of the more watery veggies, can
allow the slow-cooking process to proceed without adding extra water,
which tends to dilute the natural flavors. Whether or not you add the water,
flavor is best when you allow the braising liquid to almost evaporate,
creating a "glaze" of concentrated flavor.

2	tablespoons	olive or canola oil
1	tablespoon	ginger (optional)
1	small	onion, cut in ¾-1-inch chunks -and/or-
1	tablespoon	garlic, minced
3	cups	two or more of the following, cut in 1-inch chunks or cubes: carrot, rutabaga, parsnip, celery, daikon radish, turnip, celeriac, parsley root, peeled winter squash, beet (but be prepared for pink!)
¼	teaspoon	sea salt
	small amount	water or stock, as needed
½	teaspoon	your favorite dried herbs (or 1 tablespoon fresh)

Heat oil in a large skillet over medium heat. Add ginger, if
used; sauté for 20-30 seconds. Add onion, sauté until translucent. Add diced vegetables and salt, stir well and sauté for 2-3
minutes, adding garlic near the end to avoid browning. Add
any dried herbs used, and water or stock if liquid drawn out of
vegetables isn't enough for simmering. Cover and reduce heat
to medium-low; simmer until vegetables are very tender, about
20-30 minutes. Add any fresh herbs during last 5-10 minutes
of cooking.

4-6 servings

Use your imagination in a child-like game to help you appreciate the importance of good food and intelligent nutrition. Imagine you are your stomach or liver or heart, for example. Playing the role of your heart, you may for the first time realize what it is like to have to stand by and watch your vessels slowly fill with fatty substances. Is it any wonder if at times you try to get your feeder's attention by crying out in pain? As your stomach, you find yourself wincing in revulsion as an endless variety of harmful chemicals are dumped into you, chemicals that may prolong the shelf life of a food, but that only burn and revolt you. As your liver, you feel a horror at what flows into you and a guilt at what flows out of you. You feel you are betraying your responsibility to the rest of the body as you send it impure blood it is trusting you to have cleansed. Childish game? Perhaps.

KALE WITH PEANUT SAUCE

Young and tender kale, deep green and fresh from the harvest, is one of the best reasons I know to eat leafy green vegetables. At its peak of flavor and sweetness, this vegetable, like collard greens of similar quality, may be simply steamed and appreciated without any seasoning at all. A bit of lemon juice helps with absorption of their valuable iron content, and a touch of clarified butter, or ghee (see p. 70) is always welcome. Here, the goddess of greens is dressed with a simplified version of a traditional Indonesian sauce.

1	bunch	fresh, tender kale or collards
⅓	cup	water, or just enough to cover the bottom of skillet
1	medium	onion, sliced thinly
		-or-
6	cloves	garlic
½-⅔	cup	Spicy Peanut Sauce (see p. 103)
		chopped roasted peanuts (optional)

Clean greens (see next page). Heat water to a boil in a large skillet or saucepan; add onions or garlic and greens to the pan; bring liquid back to a boil, then reduce heat to medium-low; cover and simmer until tender. Time will depend on freshness and age of kale; check after 3-5 minutes to see if thickest stems are tender. (Pull a piece out of pan, cool under running water and taste.) Serve hot with 2-3 tablespoons of sauce on each serving. Use chopped peanuts, if you wish, for garnish.

4-6 servings

*P*lay a variation on the game suggested in the previous reflection. Identifying yourself as your stomach, what does it feel like when you are routinely fed only excellent foods that suit both you and the rest of your body? How do you feel as your liver when you are called on to cleanse from the blood only what you were designed to cleanse and when you are always able to send a genuinely purified stream of blood out to the rest of the body? Imagine what you feel as your heart when you see that your vessels have remained clear, your muscles strong and evenly pulsing year after year. Is it any wonder that your whole body is able now to send uninterrupted messages of lightness and well-being to your mind and spirit?

HOW TO CLEAN GREENS

Many people think that an occasional salad or bowl of steamed broccoli fulfils their nutritional quota for leafy green vegetables. These certainly help provide valuable nutrients, but cannot offer the kind of nutritional energy found in properly cooked, dark green leafy vegetables. Of course, many leafy greens are delicious eaten raw, and provide enzymes and nutrients which would be otherwise lost to heat. But for the more fibrous and/or bitter varieties, cooking not only enhances digestibility and flavor, it concentrates the potent energy of what would be an unmanageable amount of raw food to eat.

You can probably find some varieties in the freezer section at your local market, already cleaned and partially-cooked, but to make the most of the fresh, seasonal "cooking greens" available in your area, learn to clean them efficiently and cook them well. As you mindfully attend to the task at hand, give thanks for these gifts of life, and your ability to be here now.

This method may not be exactly what your grandmother showed you, but I think it works well. Occasionally, you'll find a bunch of greens, usually collards, which are few, flat and large enough that washing each individual leaf is practical. Most greens sold by the bunch are best washed as described below.

1-4	bunches	turnip, mustard, collard, kale, only green ones, not the pale kohlrabi, rape, beet and endive, chard & spinach, all alive!

Before removing tie or band, cut off lower 2 inches of stems. Untie 1 bunch of the greens; spread leaves out with stem ends all pointing in one direction; remove any bruised or yellowed leaves or weeds; inspect leaves to see if sand or dirt is loose or dried on the leaves. If dried on, you'll need to rinse each leaf individually, brushing or rubbing to remove dirt. If dirt or sand is loose, gather bunch together again and cut remaining, tender stems in 1-inch pieces. Transfer greens and stems to a clean sink and repeat with other bunch. Fill sink with cold water; swirl, then allow to rest briefly so dirt or sand will settle to bottom of sink (greens will float). Gently lift greens off surface of water and remove to a colander. Repeat, then check to be sure greens are no longer gritty before proceeding. Some greens require a third rinsing.

Note: To make the most of your water, cooking fuel and time in the kitchen, cook more than you need...and freeze or refrigerate the rest for quick meals throughout the week. Consider saving your rinse water for the compost pile!

*Y*ou can play yet a third variety of the game suggested on the previous two pages. Imagine what it feels like in a body once abused by smoking, chemicals, and eating unhealthy fast foods, when at last there is tangible evidence of love and a change of habits. Wholesome foods, clean air and pure water are being sent into it as consistently now as poisons were given to it formerly. Every part of your body is busy purifying and reinvigorating itself. The lungs are clearing of black residue, the blood vessels of obstructions, the stomach of burns, the liver of poisons. Now, truly, is the body getting ready to help the mind and spirit dance!

MUSTARD OR TURNIP GREENS WITH ALMOND BUTTER SAUCE

If you don't think you like these greens, try this method! Because of their pungent or bitter flavor, they benefit from blanching; this also reduces the volume so that they are more easily seasoned in a single skillet. Unless greens are too mature, they should still be bright green when finished cooking. This ensures both eye appeal and nutritional potency. Buy extra greens when locally-available and super-fresh, then freeze for later quick use. Or buy them frozen, already blanched and chopped.

6	quarts	water
2	bunches	turnip or mustard greens
1-2	tablespoons	olive or canola oil or clarified butter for sautéing
1	medium	onion, diced or sliced (or 4 cloves garlic, minced)
	to taste	naturally-brewed soy sauce or salt
1	batch	Almond Sauce (see next page)

Bring water to a rolling boil in a large pot. (If pot is not large enough for this amount of water, use less and blanch greens in 2 batches). While water comes to a boil, prepare greens (see How to Clean Greens, p. 48). Add greens to boiling water, submerging with a slotted spoon or the bottom of a stainless steel colander; cook 2-3 minutes, or until greens are almost tender, but still bright green. Drain and rinse with cold water to cool if not using immediately. Before sautéing, press out excess liquid and chop into bite-sized pieces.

Heat oil in a large skillet over medium heat; add onion or garlic and sauté until onion is translucent, about 2 minutes, or 15-30 seconds for garlic (avoid browning). Add chopped greens and stir well; sauté until hot, add soy sauce or salt, stir well and cover; reduce heat to medium-low; cook until greens are tender. Serve with Almond Sauce (see next page), as is, or with lemon juice.

Quick Variation: Substitute 3 (10-ounce) boxes of frozen greens for 2 bunches fresh, and/or omit the sauce.

6-10 ⅓ cup servings, depending on size of greens bunches and whether or not onion is used

*W*hen your body complains to your mind in the only way it can, by pain, you will do well to listen closely. Respond if you will, and as you sometimes should by way of crisis intervention, with this or that medical treatment, but not before you pause and open your awareness to hear what it is telling you. Just as a pain in your leg informs you that sitting on it uncomfortably folded under you is unsatisfactory and must be changed, so do discomfort and pain anywhere in your body carry a message about what you are doing amiss to it. So-called miracles of healing have happened to many who have learned to listen attentively to their bodies and change their treatment of it accordingly.

ALMOND BUTTER SAUCE OR SPREAD

Adds a rich and nourishing touch to green vegetables. You might like it on whole grains, as well.

½	cup	almond butter, smooth type
2	tablespoons	lemon juice
1	clove	garlic, minced (optional)
1	tablespoon	naturally-brewed soy sauce (or ¼-½ teaspoon salt)
¼-½	cup	water, as needed

Combine all ingredients except water in a small mixing bowl. Add water a bit at a time and stir with a whisk until thickened and smooth. Continue to add water while stirring until mixture reaches sauce consistency; the amount needed may vary with different brands of almond butter.

Note: When chilled, this sauce thickens and becomes a savory spread for rice cakes, crackers or toast!

about 1 cup

*T*he increased gentleness that always comes with growing consciousness is your real power. As long as you see yourself as fragile and insecure, you will be anxious to preserve an imaginary "power," and you will be defensive, hypersensitive, eager to please, competitive, blaming of others and at times cowardly.

*W*henever you are most eager to preserve your power is exactly when you most often give it away. In anxiety to look good, to gain approval, to avoid conflict which might harm you, you will find yourself trading off your integrity, your honesty, your strength, your composure, your independence. In so far as you understand and experience who and what you Are, on the contrary, you find yourself relaxing, able to stand firm with an infinitely gentle sweetness, and never again, like the man in the ancient Bible tale, selling your birthright for a simple pot of porridge.

ITALIAN-STYLE SPINACH OR LAMBSQUARTER WITH GARLIC AND TOFU

This dish is based on the traditional Italian version with eggs. It is my favorite way to eat spinach, or its wild cousin, lambsquarters (chenopodium album), which I think tastes even better if cooked properly. Goosefoot and Pigweed are other common names for this plant, whose tiny, black nutritious seeds were used by native Americans and Europeans as a flour or meal for breads. One cup of the cooked leaves supplies 400 mg. calcium! Serve this with your favorite pasta dish, or use it as a base for Corn Polenta with Tomato-Basil Sauce (see p. 96).

3	tablespoons	extra virgin olive oil
2	tablespoons	fresh garlic, minced
1/2	pound	firm tofu, drained and crumbled
1/16	teaspoon	turmeric (optional)
1 1/4	pounds	fresh spinach, washed and trimmed -or-
6-8	cups	loosely-packed tender lambsquarter leaves and stems, harvested from the tips of the most recent growth of the plant, washed and trimmed
1/4	teaspoon	sea salt, or to taste
1/4-1/2	cup	water, as needed

Heat oil in a large skillet over medium heat. Add garlic and sauté 15 seconds; add crumbled tofu and turmeric; stir well. Add spinach or lambsquarters and salt; raise heat to high, add 1/4 cup of the water; reduce heat to low as water begins to boil. Cover and simmer until greens are tender, stirring once during the cooking to be sure they cook evenly. Add more liquid only if needed to keep ingredients from sticking; when greens are tender, remove cover and cook until liquid is evaporated.

Quick Variation: Use 2 (10-ounce) packages frozen spinach, thawed and drained, instead of fresh greens.

4-6 servings

MSIQUATASH

This original native American Narrangansett name, meaning "fragments", has become "succotash" in modern English. It is another of many examples of traditional dishes which wisely combined incomplete, but complimentary vegetable proteins, resulting in complete usable protein with values greater than the sum of the parts. I like this dish because I can make it quickly and easily without much chopping; frozen cut corn and bright green limas are very convenient. Omit the onion if you want to save more time.

1	tablespoon	olive oil
1	medium	onion, diced (optional)
1	(10-ounce)	package frozen lima beans
1	teaspoon	fresh thyme leaves (or ¼ teaspoon dried)
½	cup	water or stock
2	cups	(12 ounces) fresh or frozen cut corn

Heat olive oil in a large skillet over medium-high heat; add onion, if used; sauté for 1 minute.

Add lima beans, thyme and water or stock; Bring liquid to a boil, stirring to separate frozen beans; reduce heat to medium-low and cover; simmer 3-5 minutes. Add corn and stir well; bring liquid back to a simmer; cover and cook until corn is tender, about 3-4 more minutes. Serve as is or with Spiced Roasted Pepitas and Sunflower Seeds.

about 4 cups

Note: Use any leftovers for Salad of Succotash with Red Pepper Vinaigrette (see p. 16).

A Chippewa medicine man smiled compassionately when he was asked where Native Americans get their power over illnesses, weather and other natural phenomena, a power that has so often been demonstrated and documented among nature-based societies. The explanation he gave could as well have come from Meister Eckhart in Medieval Europe or Lao Tsu in China six centuries before our modern era. He explained that this power is not magic—"Magic is not magic if you understand it"—but a simple use of forces that are a part of Nature and present for all of us to use at all times if only we become aware of who and what we Are. To underline this point, Jesus once reminded the western world that if someone with awareness were to tell a mountain to be moved, it would do so.

BRAISED BRUSSELS SPROUTS WITH PARSLEY ROOT (YES, PARSLEY ROOT!)

Once, while shopping for produce, I was asked by a Jewish woman who'd been searching the racks if I'd seen any parsley root. I said no, not in a while, and wondered what she needed it for. Chicken soup, she said - her mother always used it, and any chicken soup worth its salt had to be made with it! I never knew that. So the next time I saw it, I bought some and cooked them as below. The contrast of shapes in this dish is striking, and the flavor very comforting. I don't remember her name, but I thank that woman now and then for sharing her wisdom. I wonder if her mother ever made it this way.

1	teaspoon	canola or toasted sesame oil
		-or-
1	tablespoon	clarified butter (see recipe for Ghee, p. 70)
8	or so	young parsley roots, 3-4-inches long
³/₄	pound	brussels sprouts, tough bottoms and yellowed or bruised outer leaves removed
¹/₄	teaspoon	sea salt (optional)
1	small	red bell pepper, core and seeds removed, diced
1		fresh lemon, juiced (optional)

Wash vegetables, scrubbing parsley roots well. Trim off tops and bottom tips of roots, if tough, and peel if desired. Cut lengthwise in half; cut each half in quarters, then eighths. Cut each brussels sprout in half through the bottom. Heat canola oil or butter over medium-high heat. Add parsley roots; sauté for 3-4 minutes, or until beginning to brown lightly. Add brussels sprouts and salt, if used; sauté for 1 minute, stirring occasionally. Add bell pepper and add about ¹/₄ cup of water. Bring just to a boil, then reduce heat to medium-low, cover and simmer until vegetables are tender. Sprinkle with lemon juice, if desired, and stir again before serving.

4-6 servings

SAUTÉED RUTABAGAS WITH GARLIC AND CHERVIL

Rutabaga, in the pantry hanging basket
sprouts forth its life - green leaves, despite surrounding wax.
"I live!" it says . . . "for those who care to understand
this Gift I have to offer."

There is nothing quite like the sweet and hearty taste of a well cooked rutabaga, or "swede", as they are also called. Resulting from a cross between turnip and cabbage in the Middle Ages, this pale yellow root is higher than turnips in calcium as well as vitamins A and C. In most markets, they're sold with a thick coating of wax which must be peeled off. They are usually good even when large, unlike the turnip which gets spongy and bitter. Let bite-sized chunks braise slowly if you can, otherwise, shred and quickly stir-steam. They're delicious either way.

1	(4-inch)	diameter rutabaga
1-2	tablespoons	olive oil or ghee (see p. 70)
1/4	teaspoon	sea salt
4-6	cloves	garlic, minced
1/4	cup	water or stock
1/4	cup	fresh chervil or parsley, chopped

Use a carrot peeler to trim wax off rutabaga. To dice: hold it first on its side and cut a thin slice off one side to allow it to rest on its side without rolling. Cut in 1/2-3/4-inch-thick slices, then stack several slices at a time and cut similarly thick slices, creating thick strips. Turn these and cut again to dice into bite-sized chunks. Heat oil or ghee in a skillet over medium heat; add rutabaga and sauté, stirring occasionally, until it begins to brown - about 5-10 minutes. Add salt; stir well. Continue to sauté until liquid begins to be drawn out of rutabaga. Add garlic, sauté until it begins to turn brown; add water, reduce heat to low and simmer until tender, about 20-30 minutes. Add more water if needed to prevent sticking. Add parsley or cilantro during last few minutes of cooking.

Quick Variation: To reduce cooking time, use a bit more water and cook over medium-low heat, or shred, rather than dice, the rutabaga, using a box grater or food processor.

4 servings

Medieval philosophers said "Good is diffusive of itself." So it is, but not only as applied to the Source Being. It applies to your life as well. The Eternal Source, who diffused Life and Goodness by out-pressing (creating) a universe, still diffuses Life and Goodness here and now as it continues to express Itself as yourSelf! When you begin to realize the Goodness you share and by essence Are, you will begin to diffuse it everywhere and in all you do. No longer will it be a struggle to control your tongue, to respect others, to be gentle.

GRILLED ONIONS WITH HERBED APRICOT-MUSTARD SAUCE

These are good both grilled over hot coals or broiled in the oven.

| 2 | medium | white or yellow onions |
| ⅓ | cup | Herbed Orange or Apricot-Mustard Sauce (see p. 22) |

Peel, then slice off core end of each onion. Cut into ½-inch thick slices. In a large glass, ceramic or stainless steel pan, spread half of the sauce. Arrange onion slices on sauce, then spread remaining sauce on each onion. Allow to marinate at least 30 minutes. Pre-heat grill or oven broiler. Brush hot grill with a light coating of oil before placing onions on grill (lightly oil a broiler pan if oven-broiling). Baste onions occasionally while cooking with sauce used for marinating. Cook 5 minutes on each side, or until tender and browned nicely.

4 servings

FRAGRANT POTATO AND BROCCOLI SKILLET HASH

A nice way to use leftover baked potatoes. The cilantro is borrowed from the cuisine of India, where it is added in some recipes several times throughout the process, resulting in subtly different flavor contributions for each addition. In this case, the difference between the simmered and raw cilantro used as garnish is not so subtle! Try this, then use your imagination to create your own version with other vegetables and seasonings. I like this dish for breakfast, with or without eggs; it also complements seafood, poultry and meat dishes well. Add a dressing to the chilled leftovers for an unusual potato salad!

2	tablespoons	vegetable oil
		-or-
¼	cup	water
1	medium	purple onion, peeled and diced or sliced ½-inch thick
1	medium	gold or red bell pepper, diced or sliced ½-inch thick
¼	teaspoon	salt (optional)
5	small	-or-
3	large	baked potatoes, cooled, quartered lengthwise and cut in ¼-inch slices
1	cup	-or-
1	bunch	broccoli florettes, about 1-inch of tops (save stems for a stir-fry; see p. 99)
½	cup	cilantro, rinsed well and chopped
½	cup	water or stock

Heat oil or water in a large skillet over medium-high heat. Add onion and pepper with salt, if used, and stir well. Sauté or simmer until onions are translucent and peppers are tender, stirring occasionally, 2-3 minutes. Add potatoes, broccoli and all but one tablespoon of the cilantro, stirring well to evenly mix ingredients. Add water or stock and turn heat to high. Bring liquid just to a boil, then cover and reduce heat to medium-low and simmer until broccoli is tender, about 3- 5 minutes. Garnish with remaining cilantro and/or grated carrot for a bright touch of color.

about 5 cups; 4 to 6 servings

*T*t will be a breathtaking vision when you begin seeing yourself in the full context of your seen and unseen Universe. Here you are, a thinking, feeling, aspiring and at times somewhat confused and fearful individual in a body. You stand in a great cosmos trying to figure out your meaning and the means you must find for your safety and fulfillment. There are billions of bits of data to compute! And yet, if you will but quiet down daily and be patient, you will find yourself smiling and feeling an unbelievable degree of comfort. *You are not alone!* You are not separate from any of that which is all about you, and you have no need to gain anything. You are integral to this complete picture. You are One—perfectly and securely One— with It All.

JERUSALEM ARTICHOKES SIMMERED WITH ONIONS AND FRESH THYME

This delicious vegetable comes from a wild species of sunflower which was cultivated extensively throughout North America by native peoples. Early settlers enjoyed it, too, and exported the plant to Europe. Several years ago, I picked up a package of the knobby brown tubers at a local store. After joyfully consuming most of them, we planted 10 or so ½- inch pieces in a small plot of loose, unimproved soil. Each summer, they slowly stretch upward, eventually reaching a height of 8-10 feet before blooming their small sunflower in Autumn. Since then, we've harvested a nice little crop each winter after the first frost with very little maintenance. They do spread, and are difficult to remove completely, so be sure to plant them where you'd want them to stay.

"Jerusalem" was the English corruption of the Italian "girasole" which meant "turning to the sun." The surname resulted from the fact that the flower buds were eaten in a manner similar to the Artichoke.

2	pounds	Jerusalem Artichokes
2	tablespoons	vegetable oil or clarified butter
		-or-
		water
1	medium	onion, peeled and diced ½-inch
	pinch	sea salt
1	tablespoon	fresh thyme leaves
		-or-
½	teaspoon	dried thyme
½	cup	water or stock

Scrub Jerusalem Artichokes well and trim off any fibrous roots, bruises or dark spots. Cut into similar-sized chunks about 1-inch in diameter. Heat oil, butter or water in a large skillet over medium-high heat; add onion and salt; sauté or simmer until onions are translucent. Add thyme and sunchokes and stir to blend well. Add water or stock, bring just to a boil; cover and reduce heat to low. Simmer for 10 - 20 minutes, or until sunchokes are as tender as you like them.

6-8 servings

---

*Y*ou Are. You Exist perfectly. You have absolutely, metaphysically, nothing whatsoever to gain—even if you may still have everything to remember. Your Life is that Indivisible Life that Is All: all Abundance, all Joy, all Security, all Okayness. Your potential, your purpose, your adventure in this world is to *realize* that all of this is true. And then to experience it. You don't have to acquire it. You are not invited to go get it, but simply to recognize it.

*Y*ou are real with the Reality of all ages and all Being. You Exist with the Existence that expresses as puppies and kittens, sharks and orcas, cabbages and kings, worms and heroes, criminals and stars, and galaxies and rocks and gems. As men covered with sores and individuals who hire out their bodies. You share Being with towering cedar trees and English flower gardens. And "God looked out and saw that all of it was good."

CRUSTY ONCE- OR TWICE-BAKED POTATOES WITH MARJORAM, MUSHROOMS AND LEEKS

This dish owes its distinctive taste to Marjoram, which grows wild in the Mediterranean. Its name is Greek, meaning "joy of the mountains." Herbalists say an infusion of the fresh herb helps relieve upset stomach, indigestion and headaches. Perhaps that's why this dish seems calming. For simple, daily fare, serve over steaming hot potatoes; if you're in the mood for fancier fare, try the twice-baked variation!

4	medium to large	baking potatoes, evenly-sized
2	tablespoons	olive oil or butter
1	bunch	leeks
¼	teaspoon	sea salt
8	ounces	fresh button mushrooms
1	tablespoon	fresh marjoram (or 1 teaspoon dried) black pepper, to taste
1	tablespoon	grated Parmesan cheese or yogurt (optional)
¼	cup	chopped, roasted walnuts (optional)

Preheat oven to 400°. Scrub potatoes, removing any sprouts. Lightly coat with 1 teaspoon of the oil or butter. Use a fork to pierce the skin; bake on an oven rack for 40 to 60 minutes or until tender.

Prepare leeks: cut off root end, remove any wilted or bruised outer leaves, then cut off (and compost!) the leaves 2 inches above white part. Slice in half lengthwise and thoroughly rinse under cold running water to remove any sand or dirt. Slice ¼-inch thick, crosswise. Prepare mushrooms: use a brush or towel to remove dirt; trim ¼ inch off bottom of stem and chop coarsely. Heat remaining oil or butter in a large skillet over medium-high heat; add leeks and salt. *Note: If using dried marjoram, add it now.*

Sauté, stirring occasionally until leeks are wilted. Add mushrooms and fresh marjoram; stir well and cover; reduce heat to low and simmer 5 minutes or until leeks are tender. Remove cover; continue to cook until liquid is almost evaporated. Season to taste with salt and pepper. Serve over hot baked potatoes; add cheese, yogurt or walnuts if you wish.

Twice-baked: While potatoes are warm, slice in half lengthwise; use a spoon to remove pulp, keeping shells intact. Beat with a mixer or whisk, adding

Continued on next page

*W*hen the young Jewish prophet from Nazareth talked about a joy inexpressible and a peace no one can take from us, he was speaking from that same Divine Consciousness that had looked out over "creation" and approved of it as good, as an outpressing of Itself. It was this overarching awareness that Jesus and other spiritual masters around the world told us we have all inherited and that they urged us to recall.

*T*o the degree that you consciously recognize the true Nature of your Life, virtue becomes as natural and unstudied as is your heartbeat. Your obsession now becomes that others, too, may come to realize that they are already infinitely and eternally abundant and okay. You are beginning to dance, and you long that others will come to share your newfound delight.

CRUSTY ONCE- OR TWICE-BAKED POTATOES

Continued

water, milk or stock to get thick, fluffy mashed potato consistency. Stir in mushroom-leek mixture; add grated cheese if desired; season to taste with salt and pepper. Spoon into the potato "jackets"; bake again at 400° until tops are lightly browned.

4 servings

BAKED SWEET POTATOES WITH ROASTED PECANS AND EASY CINNAMON-ORANGE "SAUCE"

If you haven't eaten a freshly-baked sweet potato adorned simply with a few roasted pecans, please do. Such a meal usually leaves me wondering why it's been so long since the last time. If you prefer yours a bit dressier, but don't have time to make sweet potato casserole, try this recipe. It enhances the tuber's natural sweetness with extra spice and tang, and adds protein-rich, satisfying but unsaturated fat.

Freshly-baked sweet potatoes are best for this dish, but you may use the same sauce on whipped potatoes which have been reheated.

4	medium	sweet potatoes
¼	cup	pecans, chopped coarsely
	dash	ground cinnamon
¼	cup	orange juice concentrate, thawed

Bake sweet potatoes as described in An Ovenful of Simple Veggies, p. 44. Roast pecans in a regular or toaster oven for 5-10 minutes at 350°, or until fragrant and lightly browned. Slice halfway into each potato with a lengthwise cut, peel back skin a bit and fluff insides with a fork. Sprinkle cinnamon, then 1 tablespoon juice concentrate evenly across each potato. Top with roasted pecans. Give thanks for simple pleasures.

Variation: Reheat and mash or whip unsweetened, canned sweet potatoes with juice concentrate and cinnamon; add pecans to each serving.

4 servings

GINGERED ARAME WITH CARROT AND BURDOCK

Like other vegetables of the sea, arame is a potent source of trace minerals, as well as calcium and iron. Its mild flavor and exotic appearance make it a good choice for a first taste of this nutritious family of foods. Though they are commonly consumed in a variety of processed foods in the U.S., sea vegetables are not appreciated nearly as much here as they have been for thousands of years by coastal cultures throughout the world. Today, their ancient forms may offer a timely gift to help us balance with our environment. The burdock is optional; it adds an earthy flavor, is rich in iron and known in Japan and China for its strengthening qualities.

1	cup	dried arame (hijiki may be substituted, but has a stronger taste)
2	teaspoons	canola oil
1	tablespoon	fresh ginger, minced
½	cup	burdock root, scrubbed well and julienne-cut ¼-inch thick (optional)
1	medium	carrot, shredded or julienne-cut
1	medium	onion, sliced thinly
¼	teaspoon	sea salt
1½	cups	water
	to taste	naturally-brewed soy sauce or sea salt

Spread arame out on cutting board and remove any small seashells. Transfer to a bowl and fill with cold water; swirl vigorously to loosen any sand. Allow to rest 5 minutes. Lift arame out of the water and drain in a colander; reserve water. Heat oil in a non-reactive skillet or saucepan over medium heat. Add ginger; sauté for 20 seconds; add burdock, stir well and sauté for 3-5 minutes, or until almost tender. Add carrot, onion and salt; sauté until onion is translucent. Add arame, stir well to mix vegetables; add water to just cover, slowly pouring reserved soaking water out of bowl, leaving any sand behind. Bring to a boil; reduce heat to a simmer, cover and cook for 15 minutes. Add soy sauce or salt to taste and simmer 5 more minutes. Garnish with roasted sesame seeds (see p. 124).

4-6 servings

*E*verything in the spiritual life can be counterfeited. With the right temperament or discipline, you are capable of constraining yourself to be patient, or forcing yourself to act kindly and piously. The pity is that institutional religion, bent on recognizable conformity, will more often than not be satisfied with that! Its leaders may remonstrate with you about the regularity of your attendance or the adequacy of your tithe, but almost never will they be concerned about your inner state. Know that it is you who will be the loser if you let yourself be lulled or flattered into judging your life by criteria aimed at conformity. It will be you who will be the loser, not they.

SAUTÉED CARROTS AND PARSNIPS WITH PARSLEY

Though parsnips look like white carrots, they are usually much sweeter, with an earthy, nut-like flavor. Gathered from the wild in ancient Rome, they eventually were cultivated extensively in Europe and brought to North America by the early settlers. They grow best in climates where their sweet flavor is developed by near-freezing temperatures. Their natural sugar content is so high that they will brown when sautéed.

1	tablespoon	canola oil or ghee (see p. 70)
3	medium	parsnips, trimmed and peeled, cut in ¼-inch rounds
2	large	carrots, trimmed and peeled if desired, cut like parsnips
¼	cup	water
¼	bunch	parsley, chopped
1-2	teaspoons	lemon juice

Heat oil in a large skillet over medium heat; add parsnips and sauté until lightly-browned, about 5 minutes. Add carrots and water, bring to a boil, cover and reduce heat to low. Simmer until carrots are tender, about 5 - 10 more minutes. Add more liquid if necessary to keep vegetables from sticking. When tender, stir in parsley and simmer, uncovered, to almost evaporate any liquid remaining to create a glaze. Stir in lemon juice and serve.

4 servings

see p. 70

o act gently is as different from eternal Gentleness as a layer of paint is from solid gold. Authentic gentleness and joy express themselves with no more effort than that of a bird in flight.

irtues come from enlightenment: enlightenment doesn't result from an accumulation of or as a reward for virtues. You don't earn holiness or enlightenment after a long struggle to pile up virtues. By sharing Eternal Being you already possess all the Holiness and Light there is in the Universe. As you come to awareness of this fact, virtues will prove to be as natural to you as are hunger and need for sleep.

HOW TO PEEL GARLIC

The benefits of this pungent member of the Allium family are well worth learning how to prepare it easily and quickly. Fresh is so much better than bottled or dried. Used for thousands of years in Chinese medicine, garlic was also used in ancient Egypt, Greece and Rome, throughout Europe as well as North America, where wild varieties still may be harvested across the U.S. Modern research has confirmed its benefit to the cardiovascular system, as well as its antifungal and antibiotic properties. I like the wonderful things it does to enhance my meals.

To get the greatest yield with the least amount of effort, the large, mild "elephant" garlic would be the choice. If you prefer the more intense flavor of regular garlic, look for the largest of these.

1 bulb	garlic, fresh

If the papery outer covering is firm and tight, use a paring knife to cut ¼-inch into the top and strip away a section of this outer layer. Remove remaining skin and pry the larger, outer cloves off the tightly bunched center cloves. This next step will save time, especially if there are lots of small, inner cloves. Holding the cluster on its side, use a sharp knife to slice off the root end which holds the cloves together. If properly done, this cut will free all the cloves at once from the root, as well as remove the tough, flat end of each. Cut the flat end off each of the larger, outer cloves freed earlier. Next, use the flat side of a wide-bladed knife to press against each clove, using your palm above to exert enough pressure to slightly crush the clove. Repeat with each clove until all are crushed. Use your fingers to remove the skin from each clove; it should easily slip off if cloves were crushed enough. Chop or mince peeled cloves in a food processor, or gather them together on a cutting board and mince, using a curved-bladed chef's knife with a rocking motion.

In a Hebrew holy book we hear the Eternal One explaining Eternal thinking this way: "My thoughts are not your thoughts. As the heavens are exalted above the earth, so are my thoughts exalted above your thoughts." Nowhere is this difference more true than in the consideration of "sin." As you awaken into high consciousness, you will see that whenever you "sinned" in the past, what you were actually doing was only missing the mark. That is exactly the meaning of the word used for sin in the Greek writings of the Christian scriptures. You were scared and confused and as a result did something that was inappropriate to your true Nature. You missed the mark. You were simply off-target.

ROASTED GARLIC SPREAD OR SAUCE

The pungent taste of garlic mellows to soft, sweet mildness with some time in the oven. Delicious as is or enhanced with herbs and olive oil. Elegant enhancement for whole grain bread, crackers or biscuits. The sauce variation with a touch of lemon is a nice accompaniment for greens.

4	large bulbs	fresh garlic
1-2	tablespoons	extra virgin olive oil
1	tablespoon	fresh oregano (½ teaspoon dried)
2	tablespoons	water or stock
	to taste	sea salt and/or black pepper

Preheat a toaster oven to 375°; if you use a regular oven and don't want to waste the heat, see An Ovenful of Simple Veggies, p. 44. Cut off the top ¼-inch of each bulb of garlic to expose a bit of the center cloves. Don't cut the root end or peel off the outer skin. Brush the garlic with oil, allowing some to soak into the cloves. Bake for 45 minutes, or until soft. Allow to cool; remove the outer skin from each bulb, then separate cloves and squeeze out the soft garlic (each clove may be squeezed separately, or use the side of a wide-bladed knife to press several cloves against a cutting board, squeezing the garlic paste to one side while the skins are pressed flat under the knife). Combine with oil, oregano and liquid in a mixing bowl and stir well with a whisk. Adjust liquid and seasonings to suit your texture and taste preferences.

Variation: Substitute fresh parsley or other herbs for the oregano. For a thinner, sauce consistency, add about ⅓-½ cup water or stock; add lemon juice to taste if desired.

about ½ cup spread; 1 cup sauce

---

*A*ll those times you found yourself worried and feeling peripheral to Divine Love because of your "sins," your Source knew no such confusion and never in the slightest degree stopped being One with you. As you awaken to full awareness, you will compassionately forgive and love yourself in simple peace. You will more and more easily slough off habits of doubt that are not fitting to your Shared Life. Let *nothing* disturb you!

A smiling gentleness will come over you as you become acquainted with your true Self. Like all virtues, this gentleness will come to you; you don't have to go after it. In fact, if you do something to go after it, you won't find it, because it comes from what you *Are*, not from what you *do*.

BRAISED CELERY WITH RED BELL PEPPER

A relative of parsley, celery is a mild, cultured version of a plant which grows wild in Africa, Europe and the Mediterranean, and was used only as medicine until the 17th century. The juice has a diuretic effect so strong that herbals suggest it not be used in cases of acute kidney problems. It is surprising to find that this typically-served-raw vegetable tastes so good when cooked.

¼-⅓	cup	water or stock
1	bunch	celery
½	red	bell pepper, diced ¼-inch
1	tablespoon	fresh garlic, minced
1	tablespoon	fresh tarragon, chopped (or ½ teaspoon dried)

Cut off base and any dried, brown or bruised parts of celery; remove dark green bitter leaves; brush each stalk under cold running water to remove any dirt. Slice diagonally in 1-2-inch chunks. Combine all ingredients in a large skillet or saucepan; bring liquid to a boil, cover and reduce heat to medium-low. Simmer until celery is tender, but still green. Add extra liquid only as needed to keep vegetables from drying out; if liquid remains when celery is tender, simmer uncovered to evaporate to a glaze.

4 servings

*Y*ou do not *need* anything, and neither do you have to *do* anything. Obviously, you must continue to function in this three-dimensional world as long as you remain here, but there is a difference in *having* to do something and in doing it to dance out your Gift of Life. As you realize your true nature, you will find you have no "have-to's" left. This does not release you from adequate and timely functioning in this world; it only releases you from constraint. You are not insecure or wanting after all!

THE BASIC POT OF BEANS

Beans are an inexpensive source of high-quality protein, containing a significant amount of B vitamins, calcium, iron, vitamin E and zinc. Their protein, unlike that of animal foods, comes with lots of the water-soluble type shown to help lower cholesterol levels. When eaten as part of a diet of varied vegetable proteins and/or lean animal protein, the "incomplete" protein of beans is used efficiently. Food combinations based on this principle have evolved throughout the world among traditional diets in which meat was considered a luxury. Even so, some people find they digest beans better when eaten with vegetables, rather than grain. See what works for you. Many people avoid them because of the "gas" they experience after eating them. This method of cooking reduces the complex starches which cause this problem, and makes them very digestible. However, if you eat a sweet dessert (or even fruit) afterwards, don't blame it on the beans. If you're not used to eating them, start with small quantities and increase gradually. Although this method may look time-consuming, total elapsed preparation time is 15-20 minutes (the beans soak, sprout and cook nicely without your help). You're rewarded with an inexpensive batch of versatile, digestible beans which freeze well in small batches.

2-3	cups	dry beans
		water, 3 times as much as quantity of dry beans used
1	stick	kombu sea vegetable (optional; helps enhance digestibility)

Sort beans on a flat surface to remove rocks or other debris. Rinse briefly to remove any dirt or dust. Soak beans in water for about 8 hours.

Drain beans into a colander; rinse well and proceed with step 3 if using split peas; for other beans, allow to stand at room temperature. Rinse 2 - 3 times each day for 2 days or until beans just begin to sprout, showing a bump at one end of the bean. If you decide to delay cooking, refrigerate until ready.

Place beans (and kombu, if used) in saucepan and add water to just cover; bring to a boil. After 2 minutes of boiling, reduce heat to very low or transfer to a slow cooker set on low heat. Cover and cook for 8 to 24 hours, depending upon size of beans and texture desired. Cook longer and stir a bit more if you'd like more "gravy"; less if you prefer a distinct, firm texture for salads or spreads. Add water as necessary during cooking to keep beans just covered.

Yield: about 2½ times the quantity used for dry beans

GARLICKED GARBANZOS WITH OREGANO AND RED BELL PEPPER

These ingredients derive great mutual satisfaction and joy from their savory association. Definitely a dish to share with friends.

1	tablespoon	extra virgin olive oil
¼	cup (yes!)	fresh garlic, minced
¼	teaspoon	sea salt
2	small	or 1 large sweet red bell pepper diced ¼-inch
3-4	tablespoons	fresh oregano leaves, chopped (or use 1 teaspoon dried)
3	cups	well-cooked garbanzo beans and liquid (see p. 65)
		-or-
2	(15-ounce)	cans canned garbanzos, with liquid
	to taste	lemon juice and/or sea salt
		freshly-ground black pepper

Heat oil in a non-reactive skillet over medium heat. Add garlic and salt; sauté 15-30 seconds. Add bell pepper and dried oregano, if used. Sauté for 2-3 minutes, then add beans and liquid. Bring to a simmer, stir in fresh oregano and cook, uncovered, until liquid is reduced to a glaze. Season to taste and serve garnished with black pepper.

4 servings

The sacred literatures of our race try in a great variety of ways to share the mystic insight of our true place in the Universe and of the meaning of all that is around us. They do this by recounting countless individual, family and tribal experiences, sagas, poems, hymns, and racial remembrances. And you may be absolutely certain that the realization they have been circling ever closer will one day, with eternal necessity, be yours. One day you will move beyond all the images and stories to their inner content. But it is up to you when you do this. Ask that your light come quickly—"as the morning rising" in the words of an ancient Hebrew. "Ask and you *shall* receive," in the words of another.

"THE ANCIENT ONES"

The title refers to the Navajo meaning of "Anasazi", the name given to both a native culture of the American Southwest and the beautifully-colored purple and white heirloom type of bean cultivated in that area since 130 A.D. They are much lower in the gas-producing complex starches than pinto and some other beans. If they're not available, feel free to use well-cooked pintos, red or kidney beans.

This is a vegetable-laden version of "refried" beans, with much less oil than is sometimes used. Use well-drained beans if you want a texture dry enough to use in "portable" burritos or sandwiches - add cooking liquid if you'd like a moister consistency.

2	tablespoons	vegetable oil
1	medium	onion, peeled and diced
¼	teaspoon	sea salt
½	teaspoon	thyme, dried
1	teaspoon	cumin, ground
1	tablespoon	chili powder
3	cloves	fresh garlic, minced
1	large	green or gold bell pepper, de-seeded and diced
¼	cup	water or stock
3	cups	cooked Anasazi beans, well drained (see The Basic Pot of Beans, p. 65) -or-
2	(15-ounce)	cans drained kidney, pinto or red beans
		sea salt or naturally brewed soy sauce, to taste
		cayenne pepper or hot sauce, to taste

Heat oil over medium-high heat in a skillet. Add onion and seasonings. Stir 1 minute.

Add bell pepper and water; stir well and cover; reduce heat to medium and simmer about 2 minutes, or until pepper is tender. Remove cover and continue to cook until liquid has just evaporated.

Stir in well-drained beans and mix well; use a potato masher to mash until almost smooth - some pieces and whole beans create a pleasant texture. Season to taste. Fill whole grain wheat or corn tortillas with beans, grated cheese and tomatoes; top with your favorite salsa.

about 3½ cups

TANGY BAKED SWEDISH BROWN BEANS

These heirloom beans were brought to the U.S. in the 19th century by Swedish immigrants. This recipe satisfied a craving for the pungent flavor of mustard, which is used in greater volume here than common in baked beans. Season them to suit your preference.

3	cups	Swedish brown, navy or Great Northern beans, with cooking liquid (see The Basic Pot of Beans, p. 65)
1	medium	onion, grated or chopped finely
2	tablespoons	barley malt or molasses
1½	tablespoons	dry mustard
2	tablespoons	naturally-brewed soy sauce or dark miso (see p. 125)
¼	cup	ketchup or tomato sauce (optional)

Cook beans as directed in The Basic Pot of Beans, p. 65, until tender. Preheat oven to 350° while combining beans with remaining ingredients in a lightly-oiled casserole. Bake, covered, for one hour, then uncover and bake for 20 - 30 more minutes. Add more liquid only if needed to keep beans from drying out.

Quick Variation: Use 2 (16-ounce) cans pre-cooked beans and liquid to replace home-cooked beans.

4 servings

*I*dolatry was identified by the ancient Hebrews as the most heinous of all mistakes. They thought of it in the concrete terms of bowing before a golden calf or other bits of statuary. Idols that attract us today are of a more insidious sort. Substitute realities are counterfeit realities, for there is only One Isness, one Existence by which we all live and move and have our being —our life, our existence. There is only one Reality from which we have all received. Here, as in other traditional ideas, you must realize that this ancient Hebrew "law" about idolatry was not because a big "God's" feelings might be hurt, or because "He" decided to put us to a test. It was because—and only because—the sole Existence / Being / Nature / Isness ("God") is what we share as *our* innermost Nature. And whatever we would seek apart from our Nature could never suit us even if it did exist.

SAGE'S BEANS

The herb which gives this dish its earthy flavors takes its name from a Latin verb meaning "to save", referring to its widespread use in healing in Europe and China. Among its many attributes are included the ability to enhance mental calm, alertness and physical strength. Deep red, oblong kidney beans are nicely contrasted with the bright orange and the green of these vegetables. If you cook the beans yourself rather than use canned beans, be sure to cook until tender, but not mushy. As a side dish or stew, this preparation offers high quality protein and perhaps a touch of ancient wisdom.

1	tablespoon	olive or canola oil
2	medium	carrots
¼	teaspoon	sea salt
2	small	zucchini
2	small	yellow squash
1	tablespoon	fresh garlic, minced
3	cups	cooked kidney beans and liquid (see The Basic Pot of Beans, p. 65)
3	tablespoons	fresh sage, finely chopped (or 1 teaspoon dried)
	to taste	sea salt and pepper
3-4		scallions, thinly-sliced

Wash and trim ends from carrots and squashes; cut each in quarters lengthwise, then in ¼-inch slices. Heat oil in a large skillet or saucepan over medium heat; add carrots and salt; stir well and sauté for 2-3 minutes. Add zucchini, yellow squash and garlic; stir well and sauté until vegetables are just tender, about 3-5 more minutes. Add beans and sage, stir well and raise heat, bringing beans almost to a boil; reduce heat to low and simmer about 5 minutes. Adjust seasonings to taste; simmer 5 more minutes. Serve garnished with fresh scallions. Great with whole grain bread and Roasted Garlic Spread (see p. 63).

Quick Variation: Use 2 (15- or 16-ounce) cans kidney beans.

4-6 servings

---

*T*he core of the liberation movement among women and minorities is not that these once subjugated people are now acquiring the opportunity to be like their previous oppressors. That would simply replace sexism and racism with a charade of implied envy and shameless imitation. True liberation means that once subjugated individuals and classes of people are now finding and experiencing their *own* authenticity. When you see women's liberation at its most successful and when you see racial dignity newly recognized where it had lain hidden, recall that in the same way your own highest Nature, your truest Self lies within you and is also pressing to be liberated into unimaginable joy and love, peace and exhilaration. The first step to that liberation is that you love yourself: that you honestly *love* yourself.

GHEE (CLARIFIED BUTTER)

The process of "clarifying" butter removes the dairy solids and water from the pure butterfat. This results in a cooking fat of exquisite flavor which is very stable at cooking temperatures. According to ancient Indian Ayurvedic teachings, ghee has the capacity to help the body utilize the subtle medicinal benefits of herbs and spices. Definitely a source of saturated fat and cholesterol, it is best used in small amounts. Good with any vegetable; also delicious in Indian bean dishes and hot breakfast cereal.

1   pound   unsalted (sweet) butter

Melt butter over low heat in a small, heavy-bottomed saucepan. Use a spoon to skim off foam as it rises to the surface. Continue to cook over low heat, skimming occasionally, until butter stops making a "crackling" sound and turns light brown. Skim off any remaining foam. Remove from heat and allow to rest 5 minutes. Slowly pour the clarified fat into a clean glass jar or bowl, using an unbleached coffee filter or quadrupled cheesecloth if desired. The milk solids should stick to the bottom and sides of the saucepan. If completely clarified, may be stored at room temperature for several weeks or more; refrigerated, it will keep up to several months.

1⅔ cups

*M*ales, too, are today looking for liberation. Dominating by physical strength and macho posturing was a completely counterfeit foundation for worth. Today's "men's movement" is a plea and a plan for more adequate adequacy. Men's newly honest confessions and newly recognized needs are important beginnings as they recognize their highest value to be based on spiritual worth and inner Nature, not on posturing.

Grains, Pasta & Breads

I STRENGTHEN MY INTUITIVE AWARENESS OF MY PHYSICAL NEEDS BY CHOOSING SIMPLE FOODS, PREPARING THEM IN SIMPLE WAYS AND EATING SIMPLE MEALS.

Attuning to the needs of my body is an important aspect of receiving the love I deserve. The ability to know and provide for my nutritional needs has been dulled by consuming overly-refined and non-foods. I regain my natural, instinctive judgment by eating real foods in their most natural form and becoming aware of their unique effects on my body. I do this by preparing foods in simple ways, eating simple meals, and observing the results. Mental, emotional and physical results do present themselves, especially in the quiet of meditation.

GRAINS, BREADS AND PASTAS

Cultivated throughout the world for thousands of years, unrefined seeds and fruits of cereal grasses have provided humankind with balanced, inexpensive nourishment and helped civilizations to flourish. As a result, they have played an important role in the spiritual traditions and rituals of many cultures.

Foods made with refined grains can be fun to eat once in a while, but as daily fare, will not support life in a balanced way. When the outer bran and germ are stripped away, valuable fiber and most of the B vitamins, protein, trace minerals and vitamin E-rich oils go with them. It is these dis-integrated foods which have given grains their reputation for being "fatten-ing".

Soups and stews, salads and stir-fries, hot breakfast cereals, griddlecakes, puddings and pilafs, all make welcome homes for pre-cooked grains, so remember to cook a bit extra for a quick meal later!

WHILE YOU GET YOUR SLEEP

Some whole grains develop their best flavor and texture with long, slow cooking. These include whole wheat, barley, oats, triticale, spelt and kamut. Try this simple method. You'll wake up in the morning to the subtle aroma of gently cooked grain. Have some for breakfast with Spiced Fruit Compote (see p. 137) and soaked almonds, then save the rest for a hearty soup or stew (see pp. 25 and 31).

"Hulless" barley is a variety which, unlike types which must be "pearled", doesn't require removal of the seed coat. The resulting "whole" grain has lots more protein, vitamins and minerals, as well as lots of cholesterol-lowering water-soluble fiber.

1 ½	cups	**hulless barley**
6	cups	**water**
½	teaspoon	**sea salt (optional)**

Combine ingredients in a slow cooker set on low; allow to cook for 8 hours. Stir well once or twice near the end of cooking to create a creamier texture. Serve hot with your choice of breakfast toppings.

Variation: Add raisins, currants or other chopped, dried fruit at the beginning of cooking.

5½-6 cups

A SIMPLE POT OF RICE

Whole grain rice has its own unique balancing effect upon the body. Many varieties are now available, including short grain, medium or long, basmati, wehani, red and sweet. Like any grain, the essentials of preparation are simple: rehydrate with enough simmering liquid to get the kind of texture you like. Because grains require little attention during the cooking process, preparation time is minimal.

If you cook it in a casserole or pot which can function as a serving dish and storage container, you'll spend even less time on cleanup. Pressure cookers offer another alternative: high quality, modern, stainless steel models safely produce wonderful results with rice, especially the short grain and sweet brown rice varieties (see variations below).

1	cup	whole grain brown rice
2	cups	water or stock
¼	teaspoon	sea salt (optional)

Wash rice: in a bowl or cooking pot, stir rice and about 3 times as much water with clean hands, then pour off the water; wash again if needed until drained water is clear. Drain rice well.

Combine drained rice with liquid and salt in a heavy-bottomed stainless steel, glass or ceramic pot or casserole. Bring to a boil, reduce heat to low, then simmer, without stirring, for 40-60 minutes, or until grain is done (see below). Cooking time will depend on temperature, tightness of the lid, and variety of rice used. Remove from heat, stir lightly with a fork or chopsticks to fluff, then cover and allow to rest 5 minutes before serving. Serve with a brightly-colored vegetable garnish and/or a mildly salty condiment such as Roasted Pepitas and Sunflower Seeds (see p. 126) or Roasted Sesame Condiment (see p. 124).

Variation #1: To pressure-cook, use 1½ cups of liquid; cover and seal, bring to pressure over high heat, then reduce heat to low and cook for 40 minutes. Turn heat off and allow pressure to return to normal before uncovering, fluff lightly, then cover and allow to rest before serving.

Variation #2: For white (partially refined Basmati Rice, soak the rice in 2 cups of cold water for 20 minutes, then cook as above for 20-30 minutes, or until water is absorbed.

about 3 cups

How sad, how very sad, when a Reality that contains no reason for anything but lightheartedness and dance is so forgotten and misinterpreted as to become for many a context of fear and uncertainty! There is reason in the Universe only for joy, and yet we find religious groups—who claim to have special insights about a "God of Love"—building up arsenals of guns! We see conscientiously pious people at war with one another. Children are restrained from play; adults are restrained from play! Many are encouraged in bigotry and given more reason for fear and confusion than for joy and confidence. There is a solution to these errors, and it is close at hand to everyone. Look once again. Reconsider. Choose once again. Simply move beyond appearances. And how does one make this move? By meditation. It alone will take you beyond old habits of fear and hatred and uncertainty, for it alone will show you completely new data.

WHOLE GRAIN COOKERY TIPS

- For a fluffier, separate-grain texture, use the minimum amount of liquid needed for rehydration, bring liquid to a boil before adding grain, and do not stir during the cooking process. For a creamier texture, use more liquid, add grain to water before boiling, and stir occasionally.

- To determine how much extra liquid to use when cooking more than 1 cup of grain, follow this general guide: for each additional cup of grain used, add ¾ of the amount suggested for the first cup. For example: for 2 cups of uncooked rice, use 3½ cups liquid. For 3 cups rice, use 5 cups liquid. Amount may vary with different cooking utensils and lids.

- To test grain for doneness: check the texture of a few grains on top, then insert a utensil, without stirring, to touch bottom of pot; pry gently, then remove utensil and look to see if all liquid is absorbed. If grain is not tender and liquid not completely absorbed, replace cover and continue cooking until tender. If liquid is absorbed, add ¼ cup more liquid, replace cover and continue to cook until tender.

- When grain is done, fluff gently with a fork or chopsticks to mix, then replace cover and allow to rest 5 minutes before serving. The resting period will loosen the grain from the pot, making removal and cleanup easier.

- Roasting the grain prior to cooking, with or without a bit of oil, helps impart a nutlike flavor and firmer, fluffier texture. Simply stir over medium heat until grain begins to emit a pleasant, nut-like smell.

- Overnight soaking can enhance digestibility and reduce cooking time; this is especially helpful for grains with long cooking times, such as whole grain barley, wheat, rye, triticale spelt or kamut.

If the word meditation sounds too woo-woo or esoteric to you, let us put it another way. Give yourself time every day to recognize and consider your innermost desires and potential and then to watch as you see this clarified vision of yourself begin to manifest in your life. There! You are a meditator!

In teaching his novices to pray, an old Benedictine abbot used to give them this advice: "Pray as you can, not as you can't." The abbot was talking about meditation and he was right. Meditation is not some esoteric art you must somehow learn, not some exquisite set of steps that will, when learned, magically "lead you to God." Meditation is nothing more than learning to know consciously what you already Are! It is being as you are, not as you aren't. The old abbot was making a critically important point.

SAVORY QUINOA-VEGETABLE PILAF WITH WALNUTS

This delicious "grain" is not really a grain at all, but the fruit of a broad-leaved annual and a distant relative of spinach, beets, and chard. Modern researchers have called it "the supergrain" due to its excellent nutritional profile. Considered a source of "complete" protein, Quinoa contains more than twice as much as barley, corn or rice. It is also rich in calcium, phosphorous and iron. Because the plant naturally tolerates harsh growing conditions, it can be grown without the intensive use of water and chemicals commonly associated with production of some modern grains. As you enjoy your bowl of quinoa, know that you are supporting biological diversity, an important key to the strength of our resources in this age of vanishing species and genetically uniform crops. I like that it cooks so quickly, has a unique taste and fluffy texture.

1	cup	quinoa
1	tablespoon	vegetable oil
1	medium	onion, diced ¼-inch
1	medium	carrot, diced ¼-inch or shredded
¼	teaspoon	sea salt
1¾	cups	boiling water, chicken or vegetable stock
½	cup	walnuts
¼	bunch	parsley, chopped

Rinse quinoa in a fine-mesh strainer with cold water to remove the bitter-tasting saponin. Continue until the rinsing water no longer foams. Allow to drain while preparing vegetables. Heat oil over medium-high heat in a saucepan large enough to contain grain and liquid. Add onion; sauté about one minute, stirring occasionally. Add other vegetables; sauté 2-3 more minutes. Add drained quinoa and salt; add boiling water or stock and turn heat to high; bring liquid back to a boil, reduce heat to low and cover; simmer for 15-20 minutes. Roast walnuts in toaster oven at 300° for 10 minutes or until golden brown. Chop into ¼-inch pieces. Test grain for doneness (see p. 75), and add extra liquid if needed. When grain is done, add walnuts, stirring briefly with a fork or chopsticks to mix evenly; replace cover and remove form heat. Allow pilaf to rest for 5 minutes before serving. Garnish with chopped parsley if you wish, or stir in just before serving.

Variation: Substitute cracked wheat if quinoa is not available.

4 servings

When you learn by meditation to take account in your thinking and feeling of the unseen realities in your Universe, completely new kinds of joy and reasons for lightheartedness come into your days. Each time you pause for a moment, even an instant, to recall these newly realized dimensions, a new kind of happiness and mirth flashes through your body, mind and heart. You begin to recognize that human life is really only meant to be a dance.

Calmly spend your time with the Eternal Being by whose Existence you have been fashioned and by whose Life you now live. Finding God in that manner, you find all things. Since All Being was there all the time, so was all else. Beyond appearances, you have never wanted for anything and never can!

WILD RICE WITH SPINACH AND CHESTNUTS

Chestnuts are closer in nutritional value to grain than nuts, with only 5 percent fat and twice the protein of corn or rice. Some have suggested that this tree crop would be a wise alternative to some of the energy-intensive production of grain used for human and animal consumption in this country. I like the convenience of the dried, shelled product; the smoky flavor is delicious with greens. This may be served as a meal itself, a side dish, or a filling for poultry or squash.

¾	cup	dried chestnuts plus water to cover
1	cup	wild rice
2	cups	water or stock
¼	teaspoon	sea salt
2	tablespoons	olive oil or butter
2	cloves	garlic, minced
1	small	onion, diced
1	large	carrot, diced ⅛-inch or shredded
1	tablespoon	each fresh sage and oregano, chopped
¼	teaspoon	sea salt
12	ounces	fresh spinach, trimmed and chopped
2	tablespoons	water
1	tablespoon	prepared mustard (optional)
	to taste	naturally-brewed soy sauce (optional)

Soak chestnuts in water for about 8 hours. Drain and refrigerate until ready to use. Combine soaked chestnuts with wild rice, water or stock and salt in a saucepan over high heat. Bring to a boil; reduce heat to low and cover; simmer for 40-60 minutes, or until rice is tender. Check every 5 minutes or so after 30 minutes to be sure liquid has not evaporated; add only as needed to keep from sticking.

While rice cooks, prepare vegetables. Heat oil or butter in a large skillet over medium heat. Add garlic, onion, carrot, salt and herbs; stir well and sauté until onion is translucent. Add spinach and water; stir well; bring liquid to a boil, then reduce heat and cover. Simmer 3-5 minutes or until spinach is tender. Add chestnut-rice mixture and remaining ingredients; stir well to blend thoroughly.

Quick Variation: Use 1 (10-ounce) package frozen, chopped spinach; use ½ teaspoon each dried sage and oregano.

about 5 cups

SPICED TEFF WITH APRICOTS AND WALNUTS

If your body doesn't seem to tolerate grains well, try one of the many you haven't had yet, then cook a different one next time. Rotating among them provides a more balanced range of nutrients, as well as greater physical adaptability and flexibility.

Grown for thousands of years in the Ethiopian highlands, this grain is now being produced in the U.S.

Teff means "lost", referring to the difficulty of finding it if dropped - 150 grains of teff equal the weight of one grain of wheat! Because it's so small, the nutrient-dense germ and bran make up a much larger proportion of the seed's volume than other grains. As a result, teff is much higher in calcium, iron and protein than most other grains. I like it because the flavor is reminiscent of hot malted cereal, and the color is deep brown. Dried apricots add a mildly sweet and tart flavor. Cardamom is said to be warming, stimulating and good for indigestion.

1	cup	brown teff
4	cups	water or fruit juice
6-8	seeds	cardamom, removed from pod
¼	teaspoon	sea salt (optional)
½	cup	chopped unsulfured apricots
½	teaspoon	ground cinnamon
¼	cup	chopped roasted walnuts (or soaked almonds or filberts, see p. 12)

Grind cardamom seeds to a powder using a mortar and pestle. Combine all ingredients except nuts in a 2 or 3 quart saucepan. Bring to a boil, reduce heat and cover; simmer for 20 minutes, stirring occasionally. If not stirred, teff will settle to the bottom of the water and begin to congeal; if this happens, stir well with a whisk until smooth. After final stirring, replace the cover and allow to rest 5 minutes if possible. Garnish with nuts, or serve with milk or ghee (see p. 70) and/or sweetener of your choice.

Variation: The cardamom may be omitted; raisins or currants may be substituted for some or all of the apricots, ½ teaspoon ground cardamom may be substituted for freshly-ground seeds.

about 4 servings

Learning to meditate may be troublesome for many, but the greatness of its benefits after you have it justifies the confusion almost always attendant on its learning. What is the best advice about how to meditate? Simply this: just keep trying. And always turn towards greater simplicity whenever you meet a fork in the road.

Meditation is not clever or complicated thinking; not a whipping up of pleasant feelings; not something that is evidenced by freedom from physical discomfort; not clarity of thought. In fact, it usually is not anything you at first think it is. What you will find, as many have, is that while you were busy at your front door preparing for high consciousness as you imagined it, it had long ago slipped quietly in your back door.

WHOLE WHEAT COUSCOUS

Only recently has this grain-like pasta made from a high protein wheat been available in whole-grain form. It originated in North Africa, where a dish bearing its name consisted of a lamb stew over which the couscous was steamed in a special utensil. Preparation is as simple as boiling water, and it can be ready in just a few minutes for use as a pilaf, in soups or salads, or as a base for a stew or stir-fry.

1¾	cups	water or stock
¼	teaspoon	sea salt (optional)
1½	cups	whole wheat couscous
1	teaspoon	canola or olive oil

In a medium saucepan over high heat, bring water or stock and salt to a boil. Meanwhile, combine couscous and oil in a stainless steel, ceramic or glass container and use clean hands to rub the oil into the couscous. Pour boiling water over the couscous, stir once, then cover and allow to stand 5 minutes. Uncover and fluff with a fork to separate grains (if couscous sits too long before fluffing, it will form a solid mass and be difficult to separate). Cover to keep warm until ready to serve.

4 servings

*Y*ou may be confused as you are learning to find God within yourself and not off somewhere in a place called "heaven" as an earlier phase of human understanding taught. You will find yourself trying at first to picture where "inside" of you it is that the Source Being resides. Chest, perhaps? Heart? Mind? You could just as well be wondering if God is specially located in one of your big toes or ear lobes. You will be helped if you ask yourself this question: "Where does *Life* reside in me?" More accurately yet, ask if It resides *in* you at all, or is it rather a matter that It is present *as* you?

BLUE CORN-PECAN PANCAKES OR MUFFINS

Blue corn was brown by the native peoples of the southwestern United States, who considered it a sacred grain. Grown today from non-hybridized grain, it is higher in protein, potassium and manganese than yellow corn. Pecans lend subtle sweetness and substance to these pancakes, but may be omitted with satisfactory results. To save time, make a double or quadruple batch of the dry mix and store it in the refrigerator, then add the liquid ingredients just before cooking. We like to eat these with Mystic Pear Topping (see p. 142) or Cranberry Maple Sauce (see next page).

Dry Mix

1	cup	blue or yellow corn meal
1	cup	whole wheat or kamut flour
1	tablespoon	non-aluminum baking power
¼	teaspoon	sea salt (optional)
⅔	cup	pecans (optional)

Wet Mix

1¾-2	cups	milk (dairy, almond or soy) or water
2	tablespoons	vegetable oil
2	tablespoons	maple syrup or honey (optional)
1	teaspoon	pure vanilla extract (optional)

If using pecans, grind in a blender or food processor until just finely ground (will turn to nut "butter" if ground too long). Combine all dry mix ingredients and stir well to blend thoroughly. Refrigerate if you plan to save it for the future.

In a separate bowl, combine 1½ cups of the milk with the other wet ingredients and stir well to blend. Add wet ingredients to dry and stir well to blend until just smooth. Add extra milk if necessary to create a consistency just thin enough to pour from a ladle. Heat a well-oiled skillet or griddle until a drop of water will dance when dropped on the surface.

Ladle batter onto skillet, about ¼ cup for each pancake. Turn when bubbles form on uncooked surface and edges begin to dry. Cook on second side until lightly browned.

Variation: For great muffins, omit extra milk used to thin the batter; bake at 400° in oiled muffin tins until edges are lightly browned.

Note: If you are cooking for one or two, store the dry and wet mixes separately (refrigerated), then combine ¼ to ½ of each as needed for each batch.

12-15 four-inch pancakes

*A*fter you get beyond what was written in the preceding paragraph, you may seem for a time to lose contact with God in vagueness as you see the Presence in a more spiritual fashion. Be patient. One morning you will awaken to realize you exist and live with the only Isness there is. The mystery will be solved. You will be quite overwhelmed with joy—and you will realize that that joy is part of you forever. *That will be when you first realize that your only role in life is to dance!*

CRANBERRY-MAPLE SAUCE

*I'd never heard of this sweet and tangy topping before the rainy morning it
appeared on our stove. Somehow I get the feeling it originated long ago
somewhere near the maple woods and cranberry bogs of New England.*

1	cup	cranberries, fresh or frozen
¹/₂	cup	natural maple syrup
¹/₂	cup	unfiltered apple juice or apple-cranberry juice

Sort through berries to remove any bruised or damaged ones;
rinse well and drain. Combine syrup, juice and berries in a
small saucepan; bring to a boil, reduce heat to low and cover.
Simmer 5 minutes. Mash berries (a potato masher works well)
and continue to simmer, uncovered, over low heat until
mixture is thickened (about 10 minutes). Allow to cool.
Refrigerate up to 2 weeks.

1 ¹/₄ cups

COMFORT FOOD REVISITED

Macaroni and Cheese was a staple food for a while in college. These days, with whole grain pastas available, it can be a good source of complex carbohydrates. Corn pasta goes well with the golden color of this dish, but if overcooked tends to fall apart. Consider also brown rice pasta, Jerusalem Artichoke pasta and the darker spelt pasta. The non-dairy option is close to the original texture of the cheesy variety; vegetables add a colorful touch and round out the meal.

2-3	quarts	water
8	ounces	your favorite elbow macaroni or other pasta
1	tablespoon	olive or canola oil
1	tablespoon	garlic, chopped
8	ounces	button mushrooms, sliced 1/4-1/2-inch thick
1 1/2	cups	hot pasta water
1	teaspoon	sea salt
1	teaspoon	paprika (2 teaspoons for non-dairy version)
1/4	teaspoon	turmeric
2	cups	broccoli florettes, 1-inch long, or green peas, thawed
4	tablespoons	unbleached white flour
3/4	cup	cold water
3/4	cup	grated lowfat cheddar (or 3 tablespoons tahini)
1/4	cup	roasted red bell pepper or pimiento, diced (optional)

Bring water to a rolling boil over high heat; cook pasta according to package directions. While waiting for water to boil and pasta to cook, prepare vegetables. In a large skillet, heat oil and sauté garlic for 10 seconds before adding mushrooms; sauté, stirring occasionally for 1-2 minutes. Add hot pasta water, salt, paprika and turmeric; stir well, then add broccoli or peas. Bring to a boil; reduce heat to medium-low; simmer until broccoli is almost tender, about 3 minutes. Stir flour into cold water to dissolve; add to simmering liquid in skillet, stirring continuously until thickened and clear. Add cheese or tahini and peppers; stir well. Add drained pasta; stir to mix well. Serve with freshly-ground black pepper.

Quick Variation: Omit the vegetables and reduce water to 1 cup and starch to 2 tablespoons.

4-6 servings

*C*onsider a great boulder in a riverbed when distractions beset you as you are learning to meditate. Regardless of what flows past the rock, it simply be's. Were it human, we would say it simply smiles. At times flood waters roar over it. At others it is hit with great force by debris and logs. At still other times it is surrounded by the wash from a barnyard. And it smiles. When you begin to realize how ineffectual and unimportant your transient inner noise is, you will learn what the stone has learned in its millions of years.

EASY ONE-POT PASTA-VEGGIE MEDLEY WITH SUN-DRIED TOMATOES

Don't let the long list of ingredients scare you. This dish may be adapted to use what you have on hand, and can be on the table in 30 minutes, even less if you use frozen veggies.

4	quarts	water
1	teaspoon	sea salt
1	cup (packed)	sun-dried tomatoes
16	ounces	whole-grain or vegetable spiral pasta
2	small	zucchini, trimmed; sliced in half lengthwise, then diagonally ¼-inch thick
2	medium	carrots, sliced diagonally ⅛-inch thick
1	large	green bell pepper, sliced in ¼-inch strips
1	large	red bell pepper, sliced in ¼-inch strips
1	bunch	scallions, thin-sliced, white part separated from green
2-4	tablespoons	extra virgin olive oil
¼ - ½	teaspoon	sea salt, dissolved in 1 tablespoon water
1	tablespoon	fresh garlic, minced finely
¼ - ½	cup	fresh basil or parsley
½	can	(3 ounces) ripe olives, sliced
		Parmesan cheese, grated

Bring water and salt to a boil over high heat while you begin to wash, trim and prepare vegetables. When water reaches the boiling point, use 1½ cups of it to soak dried tomatoes in a small bowl for 10 minutes; drain and slice thinly; reserving soaking water for use in a soup. Bring water back to a rapid boil; add pasta gradually so as not to slow boiling; stir for 15 seconds to prevent sticking. Allow pasta to cook over medium-high heat until almost done while you continue to prepare the vegetables. Add zucchini, carrot, peppers and white part of scallion when pasta is 1-2 minutes from being done. While vegetables cook, stir dissolved salt into the olive oil. When pasta and vegetables are just done, drain in a colander (reserve liquid for soup stock if desired), then return mixture immediately back to the empty pot. Stir in all remaining ingredients, mixing well. Reserve some Parmesan cheese to top each serving. Enjoy it hot!

Variation: Add your favorite vinaigrette and serve chilled as a salad!

6 servings

PASTA WITH FRESH TOMATO, BASIL AND LEEKS

These flavors seem to touch somewhere deep in my soul.

16	ounces	spaghetti pasta
1	tablespoon	extra virgin olive oil
2	medium	leeks
¼	teaspoon	sea salt
¼	cup	chopped fresh basil (or 2 teaspoons dried)
3	medium	vine-ripened tomatoes, diced (peeling not necessary)
1	cup	tomato puree (optional)
	to taste	grated Parmesan cheese
		freshly-ground black pepper

Prepare the leeks: cut off root ends, leaving just a bit of core to hold leek together at the end; remove any wilted or bruised outer leaves and tips, then cut off (and save for a stock!) the green leaves 2 inches above the white part. Slice in half lengthwise, then thoroughly rinse under cold running water to remove any sand or dirt from between each layer; drain, slice off core end; slice the rest thinly in half-moon shapes. Cook pasta according to package directions; drain and return to empty pasta pot; cover to keep warm.

While pasta cooks, heat oil in a large non-reactive skillet over medium-high heat. Add sliced leeks and salt; stir well and sauté until leeks have wilted and begun to simmer in their own liquid; reduce heat to medium-low (if using dried basil, stir in now), cover and simmer until just tender, about 3-5 minutes.

Raise heat to high, add fresh basil and tomatoes, stir well and cook until tomatoes are just hot. Add tomato puree if desired. Serve tomato-leek mixture over warm pasta; top with cheese and pepper; garnish with sprigs of fresh basil.

Serves 4

*L*et all your observations be gentle, kind, unaffected, downright gracious. You will find that if you do otherwise, the words you have spoken will be there to meet you each time you turn to meditation. If you have tried to say and think positive, loving, supportive, patient, sensitive thoughts, you will find a golden warmth greets you when you turn inside. There is nothing magical here: you are just being met by the spiritual environment you have created. It is much like having a sweet or sour stomach during the night after you have eaten agreeable or disagreeable food. In both cases, you did or did not do something suitable to your Nature.

SPAGHETTI WITH ZUCCHINI-GARLIC SAUCE

Next time your garden (or your neighbor) offers you an armful of this prolific squash, use some of it to make this slightly offbeat pasta sauce. You'll notice the quantity of garlic is significant; most of it is sautéed to mellow the flavor, but some is saved for the end to ensure a supply of those qualities which are said to be lessened with cooking. Learn to peel garlic efficiently (see p. 62) so you'll be able to take advantage of it more often.

16	ounces	whole grain spaghetti pasta
2	tablespoons	extra virgin olive oil
¼	cup	minced fresh garlic
3	medium	zucchini
¼	teaspoon	sea salt
1	teaspoon	basil, dried (or 2 tablespoons fresh, chopped)
2	cups	tomato puree from organically-grown tomatoes

Cook pasta according to package directions; drain, then transfer to the pasta cooking pot and cover to keep warm until ready to serve. While pasta cooks, wash and trim zucchini, then shred with a grater or food processor. Mince garlic. In a large non-reactive skillet, heat oil over medium-high heat. Add 3 tablespoons of garlic; sauté about 30 seconds, stirring several times. Add zucchini, salt and basil; stir well and sauté until liquid begins to draw out of zucchini. Reduce heat to medium-low, cover and simmer for 2 minutes. Remove cover and simmer until liquid is almost completely evaporated. Add tomato puree, stir well and allow to simmer for 5-10 minutes. Serve over pasta with chopped fresh basil or parsley and Parmesan cheese garnish.

4-6 servings

*I*t should not surprise you that your kind or unkind, gentle or harsh, positive or negative words and deeds are there to greet you, for weal or woe, when you enter into meditation. You are in each case just sensing the spiritual environment you have been creating.

*A*s you grow in spiritual awareness, a finely honed consciousness of what loving and not-so-loving things you do, say and think will increasingly come to your attention. This is how you first become really convinced that the requirement to "do good and avoid evil" is not a matter of legal obligation, but of loving invitation and natural necessity.

VEGETABLE, NOODLE AND ALMOND STIR FRY

An excellent reason to cook extra pasta when you make spaghetti! This one-pot meal makes a quick lunch (or breakfast!) several days later. Don't limit yourself to the vegetables and quantities listed below; there are hundreds of different combinations to try. When using just the florettes of broccoli for a super-quick meal, we often save the lower stems for a dish like this; here both are used. The julienne, or "matchstick" cut works well for vegetables to be combined with thin noodles. To julienne hard vegetables, cut ⅛- to ¼-inch slabs (or diagonal slices for long vegetables like carrots and broccoli stems), then stack several of these and cut into slices again. Of course, a sharp knife is essential.

1	tablespoon	canola oil
1	tablespoon	minced, peeled ginger
1	small	carrot, cut julienne-style or shredded
½	cup	julienne-cut daikon (Chinese radish)
1	bunch	broccoli
½		gold bell pepper, quartered, then cut diagonally in thin strips
1	medium	purple onion, cut in half and thin-sliced
6-8		red radishes, thin-sliced rounds
4	cups	cooked spaghetti or soba (buckwheat) noodles (about 8 ounces dry weight)
1-2	teaspoons	toasted sesame oil
	to taste	naturally-brewed soy sauce or sea salt and/or hot sauce or cayenne pepper
½	cup	soaked almonds, chopped coarsely

Wash and prepare vegetables. Cut to separate lower 3-4 inches of broccoli stems from tender, upper stems and florettes. Peel or slice off tough skin from these; cut in julienne slices as described above. Thin-slice tender upper stems, leaving florettes about 1 inch long. In a large skillet or wok, heat oil over medium-high heat; add ginger; sauté 15 seconds; add carrot, daikon and broccoli stems with salt, sauté 2-3 minutes; add broccoli, pepper and onion with ¼ cup of water; cover and steam for 3 minutes or until broccoli is just tender. Add radishes; stir well; add cooked pasta and other ingredients to taste. Garnish with almonds.

Quick Variation: Shred root vegetables and broccoli stems with a grater or food processor.

about 7 cups, or 2-5 servings, depending on your appetites!

*Y*our ego will criticize you at first for what you see as amiss in your life as you progress in meditation. Slowly and very strongly, however, Love will convince you it doesn't make the kind of difference you have always thought it did. All that really matters is that you are or are not loving, are or are not acting according to your Nature. Obligation is not based on a law to be kept, but on your Reality to be lived.

OPEN SESAME NOODLES

This appetizer or snack can easily become a main dish. Although usually served cold in warm weather, the sauce may be served on hot pasta if you wish. Depending on how much of the spicy stuff you use, this dish may open more than just the meal. The sauce is traditionally made without the starch, which in this version helps keep the fat content down.

½	pound	thin noodles (Chinese egg, spaghettini, or buckwheat soba) cooked according to package directions, drained and rinsed to cool
1	cup	cool water, stock or shiitake mushroom liquid
½	teaspoon	crushed red chilies
1	tablespoon	arrowroot, kudzu or cornstarch
¼	cup	sesame tahini or peanut butter
1	tablespoon	fruit juice concentrate, maple syrup or honey
1	teaspoon	toasted sesame oil
1	tablespoon	wasabi (Japanese Horseradish) powder
1-2	tablespoons	soy sauce or sea salt to taste
½	small	cucumber
2		scallions
2	tablespoons	roasted sesame seeds (see p. 124)

Combine ¾ cup of the water or stock with the chilies in a saucepan. Heat to a simmer; cook, covered, over low heat for 2 minutes. In a small bowl or measuring cup, combine remaining liquid with starch; stir to dissolve. Add dissolved starch to simmering liquid, stirring continuously until thickened and clear. Remove from heat; allow to cool slightly before adding tahini and remaining seasonings. Adjust seasonings to taste, but allow a few minutes for flavors to blend before adding too much more. Peel the cucumber if waxed, cut in thin diagonal slices, then stack several slices at a time and cut these into thin strips. Cut scallions in thin, diagonal slices. To serve, pour about ¼ - ⅓ cup sauce over each serving of noodles, then top with cucumber, scallions and roasted sesame seeds.

Quick Variation: Omit the starch and simmering process: combine all sauce ingredients except the water or stock in a mixing bowl, then use a whisk to gradually stir in only enough liquid to thin to desired consistency.

6-8 appetizer or 4 main dish servings with leftover sauce for other vegetable or grain dishes!

ONION-SPELT BREAD

Spelt, a non-hybridized variety of wheat, was first cultivated over 9,000 years ago. Its gluten is well-tolerated by many who have problems with wheat. Kneading bread by hand is one of those skills which is best learned from a friend. You'll develop your own style and rhythm, of course, but your friend will greatly appreciate the chance to pass it on.

2½	cups	warm water (about 110°)
1	package	dry active yeast
¼	cup	barley malt, rice syrup or honey (optional)
½	cup	finely-chopped onion
2	tablespoons	vegetable oil
2	teaspoons	sea salt
5½ - 7	cups	whole grain spelt flour or whole wheat flour

In a large mixing bowl, stir yeast into water. Add a tablespoon of the sweetener, if used; allow to stand 5 minutes. Yeast should bubble a bit, if active. Add 3 cups of the flour; stir about 100 times; cover; allow to rest in a warm (85-100°) place for 10 minutes. Add oil, salt, remaining sweetener and onion, stir well. Begin adding a bit of flour at a time, stirring after each addition, until dough is too thick to stir and pulls away from the sides of the bowl. Turn dough out of bowl onto a lightly floured table. Sprinkle flour over the dough, then knead the dough: pick up the edge farthest from you; fold it in half toward you. With the heel of one hand resting in the center of folded edge and the other hand on top, push lightly into the center of the dough. Give the dough a quarter turn; repeat the folding and pushing motions. Add flour only as needed to keep the dough from sticking to your hands and the table. Continue to knead for about 10 minutes, or until dough is smooth and elastic and no longer sticking. Transfer to an oiled bowl, with smooth side up; lightly oil the top of the dough. Cover with a damp towel and allow to rise until almost doubled in bulk, 50-60 minutes. Punch dough down and knead lightly in the bowl to expel all the air. Cut dough into 2 equal pieces; cover with a cloth; allow to rest 10 minutes. Oil 2 5x9-inch loaf pans. Flatten each piece of dough into a ½-inch thick square shape about 8 x 8 inches, then roll up tightly to expel any air; seal edges. Place seam side down in pans with each end of dough touching ends of pan; brush top with oil and cover; place in a warm place to rise until almost double in size. Bake at 350° for 45 minutes. Cool before slicing or storing refrigerated or frozen in a plastic bag.

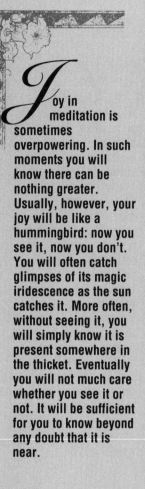

*J*oy in meditation is sometimes overpowering. In such moments you will know there can be nothing greater. Usually, however, your joy will be like a hummingbird: now you see it, now you don't. You will often catch glimpses of its magic iridescence as the sun catches it. More often, without seeing it, you will simply know it is present somewhere in the thicket. Eventually you will not much care whether you see it or not. It will be sufficient for you to know beyond any doubt that it is near.

ROSEMARY AND SAGE BISCUITS WITH GARLIC ESSENCE

Kamut, an ancient Egyptian word for wheat, is the name recently given to a grain believed to be much like that harvested as long as 6,000 years ago. It is three times the size of modern wheat, has 20-40% more protein, and is well-tolerated by many who suffer from wheat allergies.

⅓	cup	extra virgin olive oil or canola oil
1 ¼	cups	water or milk
2	tablespoons	sweetener, optional
1 ½	tablespoons	sage, dried (or 4 tablespoons chopped, fresh)
¾	teaspoon	rosemary, dried, crumbled (or 1 tablespoon chopped, fresh)
2	cups	kamut flour
2	teaspoons	non-aluminum baking powder
½	teaspoon	sea salt
2	large cloves	fresh garlic

Combine oil, water or milk, sweetener, sage and rosemary in a mixing bowl. If using dried herbs, allow this mixture to soak 15-20 minutes before baking. In a separate bowl, combine flour, baking powder and salt. Peel garlic; slice each clove into 6 thin slices. Preheat oven to 400°. Lightly oil baking sheet. Stir wet mixture well before adding to dry mix; stir together until just moistened. Use a large spoon or ¼-cup measure to drop ¼ cup portions of batter onto baking pan. Insert a slice of garlic into the top of each biscuit before baking, leaving ¼-½-inch sticking out. Bake for 15-20 minutes, or until edges begin to brown. Garlic may be removed before eating if you wish.

Variation: Add ¼ cup grated Parmesan cheese and increase liquid by ¼ cup. Whole wheat flour may be substituted for kamut flour.

12 biscuits

BUTTERNUT SQUASH BUTTER WITH SPROUTED WHEAT TOAST

One of the most consistently sweet squashes commonly available, butternut squash also yields a lot for little effort. Like any orange vegetable, it is rich in cancer-preventive beta-carotenes. Its cousin, buttercup squash, has more of a buttery flavor, and is an excellent substitute when it is sweet. This spread is good on any toasted whole grain bread, but is particularly well-suited to a type of sprouted wheat bread made without yeast, oil or sweeteners. Its natural sweetness is a result of the malting of crushed sprouts during a slow baking process. Sold frozen, it is best sliced thinly and toasted before topping with spread.

2	cups	baked butternut or buttercup squash (see An Ovenful of Simple Veggies, p. 44)
¼	cup	sesame tahini
1	teaspoon	cinnamon, ground
¼	teaspoon	mace or nutmeg
¼	teaspoon	dried ginger
⅛	teaspoon	cloves
1	tablespoon	brown rice or barley malt syrup or honey (optional)

Measure all ingredients into a mixing bowl or food processor. Puree or stir with a whisk until smooth. Refrigerate.

2¼ cups

*R*elaxing consciously into one's own Being is highest contemplation. Truly, it is finding God. It ends the search. It is the joy and peace masters have told us of. Contrary to what you may fear, this finding of Self does not in any way displace the Source Being and exalt the ego. Finding Self is quite a different thing than finding the ego! True Self discovery precisely displaces the ego and exalts "God"! Words cannot convince you of this. Understanding here only comes from experience, never from clever arguments. We acquire this sort of spiritual experience only from being quiet in meditation.

Main Dishes

I CAN LEARN ABOUT BALANCE FROM THE HABITS OF PEOPLES WHO
LIVED CLOSE TO THE EARTH.

I can learn much about food selection and preparation from the
example of traditional/ancient peoples who lived in my region or a
similar climate, for they had daily contact with the earth and the
production of their food. Their wisdom was passed down through
generations as their cuisines and healing arts evolved around simple,
locally-available and seasonal foods and herbs. Their ways can help
me adapt to my place on the earth.

MAIN DISHES

As we learn more about the effect of food on our bodies, we revise our concepts about what constitutes a "main dish". As I was growing up, "What's for dinner?" usually wanted to know what meat, fish or chicken dish would be served. Since then, scientists have confirmed that the ancient food habits of traditional cultures were healthier than those which evolved with rapid technological change since the turn of the century. In a temperate climate, this often meant that whole grains, beans and vegetables were supplemented with small amounts of animal protein, rather than served as "side dishes" to the meat. So now we look to the ethnic cuisines of the world for both wisdom and inspiration as we build healthy habits back into our lives. Fortunately, our taste buds can be happy, too.

QUICK AND LIGHT FOR A DANCING HEART

So you want to eat well today, but other demands on your time leave little for cooking. Let yourself enjoy a high-quality convenience food from the freezer or deli, embellished with fresh salad greens. Or take a few minutes to put together this meal. Based on frozen vegetables, whole grain couscous (see p. 79) and bottled roasted peppers, this dish can be ready in the time it takes the veggies to steam.

1	batch	whole wheat couscous
½	cup	water or stock
2	(10-ounce)	packages mixed frozen vegetables
½	teaspoon	coriander, ground (optional)
¼	cup	pimientos or diced roasted red peppers (or diced fresh pepper)
2-3	cloves	garlic, minced (optional)
½	cup	Simple Lemon Vinaigrette Dressing (see p. 20)
3-4	tablespoons	thinly-sliced scallions or purple onion

Prepare Couscous. Combine first three ingredients (with fresh peppers, if used) in a saucepan or skillet over high heat; bring liquid to a boil, stir veggies to separate, then reduce heat to medium-low and simmer until tender. Uncover, add pimiento or roasted peppers and garlic, if used, stir well and simmer to almost evaporate remaining liquid. Serve over hot couscous, top with dressing and onion. Relax, then enjoy.

Quick Variation: Replace Simple Lemon Vinaigrette with your favorite bottled dressing.

4 servings

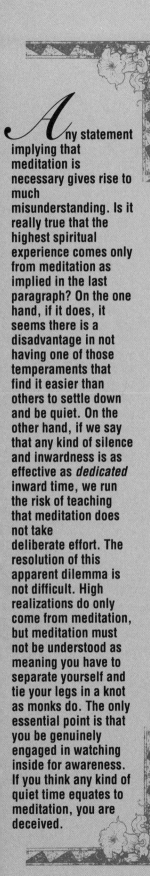

*A*ny statement implying that meditation is necessary gives rise to much misunderstanding. Is it really true that the highest spiritual experience comes only from meditation as implied in the last paragraph? On the one hand, if it does, it seems there is a disadvantage in not having one of those temperaments that find it easier than others to settle down and be quiet. On the other hand, if we say that any kind of silence and inwardness is as effective as *dedicated* inward time, we run the risk of teaching that meditation does not take deliberate effort. The resolution of this apparent dilemma is not difficult. High realizations do only come from meditation, but meditation must not be understood as meaning you have to separate yourself and tie your legs in a knot as monks do. The only essential point is that you be genuinely engaged in watching inside for awareness. If you think any kind of quiet time equates to meditation, you are deceived.

SPICY RED AND BLACK BEAN TORTILLA PIE

This dish is fun and easy to prepare! The protein values of the corn and beans complement each other, and are also boosted by the turkey (if used) and cheese. Masa flour, or masa harina, is finely-ground cornmeal soaked in limewater used to make corn tortillas. Here, it helps to thicken and set the bean mixture during cooking. Tortilla Pie is even better the next day.

3	cups	or 2 (15-ounce) cans your favorite vegetarian or natural turkey chili
1	(15-ounce)	can black beans, well-drained
1/2	cup	masa flour or corn flour
3	tablespoons	chili powder
1	teaspoon	each ground cumin and dried oregano
1/8-1/4	teaspoon	cayenne pepper (optional)
16	ounces	(2 cups) salsa
1	package	(12) whole-grain yellow corn tortillas, thawed
1/2 to 1	cup	Cheddar-type soy or regular cheese, grated
1	cup	green bell pepper, diced 1/4-inch
1	medium	tomato, diced 1/2-inch
2	tablespoons	red onion, minced
1/2	cup	sliced black olives
1-2	tablespoons	fresh cilantro, chopped (optional)

Preheat oven to 375°. Lightly oil a 9x13-inch casserole dish. Combine chili, black beans, flour and seasonings in a bowl; stir to blend well. Arrange six of the tortillas in casserole, overlapping to evenly cover bottom. Spread 1 cup of the salsa evenly over tortillas, then spoon the chili and black bean mix onto the tortillas, spreading to cover the tortillas evenly. Sprinkle half of the grated cheese over the chili mix, then layer the remaining tortillas on top. Spoon remaining salsa over the tortillas, add bell pepper, cover with lid or foil and bake for 40 minutes.

Note: The pie may be cooled and refrigerated for later use at this point. When ready to use, cover with foil and reheat until hot, then proceed.

Remove cover and add tomato, onion and olives to cover top; sprinkle on remaining cheese, return to oven and bake until cheese is melted and bubbly. Remove from oven and allow to stand for 5-10 minutes before cutting into 6 to 8 pieces. Garnish with cilantro if desired.

6 servings

You will smile and smile one day when you realize that all your worry and fretting about spiritual growth and security were unnecessary. The Reality which meditation will one day reveal to you was there all the time! You were meditating all the while, but your attention was, as it were, in the wrong part of your house. This reassurance doesn't mean you may quit trying, only that you may quit fretting. Here's a truism for you: in so far as fretting goes, meditation comes. And vice versa.

TANGY STUFFED SQUASH

This dish borrows some of the flavors of the Japanese specialty "Norimake", which uses toasted sheets of the dried sea vegetable Porphyra Tenera to enclose "sushi rice" and pickled or pungently seasoned vegetables. If you've had "sashimi", the raw seafood appetizer served at sushi bars, you've had nori. Rich in protein, vitamin A, calcium and iron, toasted nori's nutlike taste and dark color makes for an interesting garnish when crumbled or cut into thin strips. Find it at a natural food or Asian market.

2	small	acorn squash
1	tablespoon	toasted sesame oil
½	medium	onion, diced
1	small	(½ cup) carrot, shredded
4	ounces	fresh shiitake or button mushrooms (tough stems removed), sliced
¼	teaspoon	sea salt
1	cup	cooked kale, mustard or turnip greens, chopped finely
1	tablespoon	each lemon juice or brown rice vinegar and water
1½	tablespoons	wasabi (Japanese horseradish) powder (or prepared mustard)
1	tablespoon	tahini
2	cups	cooked short-grain brown rice (see p. 74)
		naturally-brewed soy sauce, to taste
2	sheets	nori sea vegetable

Preheat oven to 375°. Prepare and bake squash as described on p. 44. Heat oil in a skillet over medium heat. Add onion, carrot, mushrooms and salt; sauté until onions are translucent. Add greens, stir well and cover; reduce heat and simmer 3-5 minutes, adding just enough liquid to prevent sticking.

In a small bowl, combine water, lemon juice or vinegar, wasabi and tahini; stir well to blend. Remove vegetables from heat and mix in seasoning mixture, then rice, stirring very well to mix thoroughly. Season to taste with soy sauce. Fill each squash half with ¾ cup of rice mixture; return to the oven for 5 minutes while toasting nori sheets: hold each with your fingers or a pair of tongs and wave it over a medium-low gas flame or in a 250° oven until it becomes crisp and turns green. Place on a dry cutting board and cut lengthwise in thirds, then in thin, ¼-inch strips. Serve.

Quick Variation: Use 1 (10-ounce) package frozen spinach instead of the greens; use 1½ cups any pre-cooked or frozen vegetables instead of those used in the rice mixture.

4 servings

CORN POLENTA WITH TOMATO-BASIL SAUCE

Polenta is the Italian name for a simple cornmeal porridge. In this version, the polenta is prepared ahead, chilled and sliced, then pan-fried or broiled before serving with the sauce. Try it served over Italian-style Spinach (see p. 51).

4	cups	water or stock
½	teaspoon	sea salt
1½	cups	yellow cornmeal
½-1	cup	mozzarella cheese, grated (optional)
2	tablespoons	extra virgin olive oil for pan-frying or baking
1	(16 ounce) jar	organic tomato sauce
½	cup	chopped fresh basil (or 1 tablespoon dry)
½	cup	grated Parmesan cheese or ¼ cup roasted pine nuts
½	cup	sliced ripe olives
4	sprigs	fresh basil

Bring 2½ cups of the water to a boil in a heavy-bottomed medium saucepan. Combine remaining cold water, salt and cornmeal; add to boiling water; reduce heat to medium and stir until thickened and smooth. Mixture should be very thick, but moist enough to "settle" in the pan; add a bit more liquid if necessary. Reduce heat to very low and cover. Simmer for 25 to 30 minutes, stirring occasionally. If using cheese, stir in for the last 15 minutes of cooking. Remove from heat and allow to rest, covered, 5 minutes. Transfer to a lightly-oiled 8x8-inch glass casserole while still warm. Smooth surface with a wet spatula or spoon. Allow to cool; cover and refrigerate until ready to use (at least 1 hour). Combine sauce and basil in a small saucepan; bring to a simmer; cook 10 minutes. Remove polenta from container: loosen edges with spatula or knife, then invert container over a cutting board to allow to drop out. Use a wet knife to slice into 9 squares, then cut each square in half horizontally. Heat oil in a well-seasoned cast iron skillet or non-stick saucepan; pan-fry triangles until golden brown (or brush each piece with oil and broil on an oiled cookie sheet until lightly browned). Arrange polenta on individual serving plates; garnish with grated cheese or pine nuts, olives and basil leaves.

Variation: Try adding fresh or dried herbs or ½ cup minced onion to the polenta while it cooks.

4 servings

*Y*ou have gone far if you no longer depend on others for every bit of reassurance, encouragement and guidance you need on your path to enlightenment and fulfillment. Be careful that you don't substitute dependence on unseen guides for seen ones, as many do, thinking themselves singularly spiritual thereby. Be intimate with your unseen friends, angels and guides, yes, but don't await their guidance and reassurances as you once did that of teachers and counselors. The point, after all, is that you come to recognize and exercise your own resources, to depend on yourself, not that you just transfer your dependence from one external source to another.

SZECHUAN STIR-FRY WITH FRESH ASPARAGUS AND SWEET GOLD PEPPER

Use tofu or shrimp to create a delicious and elegant dish fit for special company: Yourself! This is actually a "stir-steam", I prefer to finish the cooking in hot liquid to avoid using an excessive amount of oil and to ensure a more tender, rather than crunchy texture. Here, the onion is added at the end to help preserve its pungency and color.

2	tablespoons	toasted sesame or canola oil
2	bunches	fresh asparagus, preferably thin
1	large	sweet orange or yellow bell pepper, cut in ¼-inch strips
1	medium	purple onion, halved, then cut in ¼-inch strips
1	pound	peeled and deveined shrimp -or-
1	batch	marinated and baked Szechuan Tofu (see next page)
2	cups	marinade from Szechuan Tofu (see next page)
2	tablespoons	arrowroot, kudzu or cornstarch
2-3	tablespoons	roasted sesame seeds (see p. 124 for roasting technique)
4	cups	cooked long grain brown rice, optional (see pp. 74 and 75)

If using tofu, marinate and bake as directed on next page. Prepare vegetables. For asparagus, gently bend each stalk to break off tough, woody ends. Compost or save them for soup. Peel the skin off the bottom 2 inches of any fat or older stalks using a peeler or paring knife. Then cut the stems diagonally into 1½- to 2-inch sections, leaving 2 inches at the tips. If the lower stems are particularly thick, separate these from the thinner, upper stems and tips.

Dissolve the starch in 1 cup of the marinade; set aside. Heat the oil in a large skillet or wok over medium-high heat. Add thicker asparagus stalks, if separated, and stir-fry 1 minute. Add remaining asparagus and bell pepper; stir-fry 1 minute, raise heat to high and add 1 cup of marinade; bring to a boil, reduce heat to medium, then cover and cook until vegetables are almost tender. Add onion and shrimp, if used, stir well; cover and cook until shrimp is pink but not tightly curled. Stir starch liquid, then add to simmering liquid, stirring continuously until thickened and clear. Serve immediately over rice or by itself. If serving tofu version, place tofu in the center of each mound of rice and surround it with the vegetables.

4 servings

If you seek your sense of okayness, your validation from others, you are making yourself dependent on something more whimsical than a summer breeze. In so far as you do this, you delay true inner freedom: you delay your heart's dancing. Make your point of reference for authenticity, for peerage, for worth, your own inner Reality. Then you will be almost there.

Your self-respect always comes back to this: your worth is based inside, not outside. It is eternally built on that part of you greater-than-which cannot be conceived: Eternal Being outpressing here as you. This Divine Life is now, and forever will be, yours by Absolute Right. And would you go through life ignoring It or being satisfied with counterfeits?

MARINATED SZECHUAN TOFU FOR STIR FRY OR APPETIZER

I like this method of preparing tofu for stir-frying because it imparts great flavor and results in nicely-browned, bite-sized pieces which don't crumble as easily as those browned in the wok or skillet. This is delicious as a side dish or party snack, too, especially if you can find the naturally-black sesame seeds to sprinkle on for rich contrast.

1	pound	firm-style tofu, drained
⅓	cup	sherry, rice wine, pineapple or orange juice
⅓ - ½	cup	naturally-brewed soy sauce
1 -2	tablespoons	sweetener (optional)
1½	cups	water
1	tablespoon	toasted sesame oil
3	or more	cloves garlic, minced
1	tablespoon	ginger, minced
1	teaspoon	crushed hot chilies (or ¼ teaspoon cayenne pepper)
1	tablespoon	black or regular sesame seeds, roasted (see p. 124 for technique)

Cut tofu in ⅓- ½-inch slices and pat dry on a clean towel. In a large mixing bowl or 9x13-inch glass casserole dish, combine all ingredients except tofu and stir well; add tofu slices and marinate at least 30 minutes, up to 24 hours.

Remove from the marinade, shake off excess liquid, then cut each slab into triangles as follows: cut each slice in half to create 2 squares; cut each square diagonally to create triangles. Preheat the oven to 425°. Place tofu on an oiled cookie sheet, brush with oil and bake for 10 - 15 minutes, or until nicely browned. Serve warm with roasted sesame seeds as an appetizer or side dish (refrigerate or freeze the marinade for another use) or use tofu and marinade as directed on preceding page.

Variation: Use more garlic, ginger or chilies to suit your tastes!

4 to 6 servings

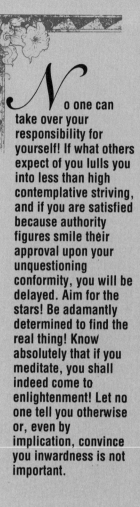

No one can take over your responsibility for yourself! If what others expect of you lulls you into less than high contemplative striving, and if you are satisfied because authority figures smile their approval upon your unquestioning conformity, you will be delayed. Aim for the stars! Be adamantly determined to find the real thing! Know absolutely that if you meditate, you shall indeed come to enlightenment! Let no one tell you otherwise or, even by implication, convince you inwardness is not important.

QUICK GRAIN AND VEGETABLE STIR-FRY

When you're short on time, this meal can be just minutes away if you have the right ingredients on hand. Pre-cooked grain or pasta, frozen (organic) vegetables, fresh or frozen peas, tofu or other lean protein, and a few basic seasonings...can all be tossed together in a single skillet or wok, making cleanup easy, too! The key to quick is keeping it simple, although this dish may be as complex as you wish. The first time you try it, use only one vegetable other than onion or garlic. Enjoy simplicity!

1-2	tablespoons	canola oil
1-2	tablespoons	fresh ginger, peeled and minced finely
1	small	onion, diced or thin-sliced (or white part of 4-6 scallions) -and/or-
1-4	cloves	garlic, peeled and pressed or chopped finely
2	cups	one or more of the following, sliced or shredded as desired: carrot, rutabaga, turnip, daikon, celery, green cabbage, peeled broccoli stems, cauliflower, asparagus stems, jicama
1-2	cups	one of the following: fresh or frozen green peas, sugarsnap peas, snowpeas or drained, cubed firm-style tofu
¼	cup	water or stock
½-1	cup	something brightly colored and/or intensely flavored, chopped: watercress, scallion tops, parsley, cilantro, purple onion, fennel leaves, red or gold bell pepper
2-4	cups	pre-cooked grain, fluffy, separate-grain texture and chilled if possible
	to taste	naturally-brewed soy sauce, sea salt, lemon juice and/or hot sauce

Heat oil in a large skillet or wok over medium-high heat. Add ginger and onion, if used; sauté for 2 minutes. Add garlic, if used, with hard vegetables; sauté 1 minute. Do not let garlic brown. Add peas or tofu and water or stock; bring to a boil; cover and reduce heat to medium. Cook 5-8 minutes, or until vegetables are tender. Add something brightly colored; cover and cook 1 minute. Add water only as necessary to keep food from drying out or sticking to pan. Add grain and stir well, continuing to cook over medium-high heat until grain is heated through. Season to taste.

Main Dishes ❦ 99

*A*fter meditation has begun to give you an experience (as distinct from a conviction) of the Presence of the Eternal One, you have yet another aspect of your adventure before you. You may for a time find it difficult to rise from this sort of experience and go off to your daily duties. This can be a difficult hurdle. It is solved only when you realize that when you leave your spiritual exercises to go to work, you leave nothing behind.

*I*t is not a possibility for Reality to be here and not "there," more here and less "there." This fact has tremendous implications for your daily living. Here is a gauge of your enlightenment: do you realize you are invited to rejoice in the experience of the Presence *always*? This is so as much when you are bagging groceries, sitting in a critical meeting, doing dishes or cleaning the cow barn as when you are seated alone and deep in contemplation.

MILLET GRIDDLECAKES (OR PILAF) WITH MUSHROOM-GARLIC SAUCE

Griddlecakes are based on the same principle as polenta, but use a whole grain, rather than meal. When cooked with a bit more water than used for dry, fluffy grain, and stirred a bit, many grains will chill in a solid form which may be sliced and pan-fried with delicious results. Another excellent reason to always cook a bit more grain than needed for today's meal.

Millet is a small, round, yellow grain used as a staple food in Africa and China for thousands of years. Gluten-free, it is higher in protein, iron and B vitamins than most common grains, and seems to provide a balancing, stabilizing influence. Though it may be cooked plain or with fruit, chopped onions are my favorite seasoning. Use the smaller amount of water if you want to serve it as a pilaf-like side dish.

1	cup	millet, rinsed and drained
¼	teaspoon	sea salt
2- 2½	cups	water or stock (less for pilaf, more for griddlecakes)
1	small	onion, diced (about 1 cup)
		olive oil or ghee (see p. 70) for pan-frying
1½-2	cups	Mushroom-Garlic Sauce (see facing page)

Dry-roast millet in a heavy-bottomed saucepan over medium-high heat, stirring constantly until it emits a nutty, fragrant smell. Add salt and water or stock and raise heat to high. While waiting for liquid to come to a boil, dice the onion and add; when liquid boils, reduce heat to very low and cover; simmer 25-30 minutes, or until water is absorbed. Check for doneness (see p. 75), fluff with a fork and allow to rest. Serve as is with sauce for pilaf. For griddlecakes, stir well, allow to cool slightly and spread into a square or rectangular container, smoothing the top before refrigerating. When chilled at least 1-2 hours, invert onto a cutting board and cut into rectangular or triangular slices. Pan-fry on an oiled or buttered cast iron or non-stick skillet until lightly browned on each side. Serve while hot with sauce. Garnish with chopped scallions.

Variation: To get the most variety from a single batch of millet, cook with the smaller amount of water and serve some as a pilaf with Roasted Sesame Condiment (see p. 124); before the leftovers cool, add a bit more water and stir well to create a very thick mashed potato-like texture; then refrigerate for use as griddlecakes another day.

3½ cups, or 4-6 servings of pilaf or griddlecakes

*Y*ou may at times experience a sense of weariness at the prospect of arising in the morning to begin another day in which you are called on to do more than just contemplate your newly realized Reality. This will be especially so when you must undertake some wearisome task with or for persons whom you find tiresome or at odds with your new insights. This weariness is an indicator of what in a previous age would have been called your lack of "purity of intention." Today, more directly and more accurately, we would refer to it as your forgetfulness of your true Nature—and of theirs.

MUSHROOM-GARLIC SAUCE

Shiitake mushrooms have been used in the folk medicine of China for thousands of years. Modern research has verified that they contain substances which combat virally-induced diseases and lower blood cholesterol levels. The taste is very distinctive. The texture of rehydrated, dried mushrooms are different than fresh; try both to see which you favor. This sauce is versatile; use it with burgers of any kind, felafel or pan-fried tofu, baked or mashed potatoes, natural meat or poultry.

1	tablespoon	olive oil or butter
8	ounces	fresh shiitake mushrooms, sliced ¼-inch thick -or-
1	cup	(1 ½ ounces) dried mushrooms, reconstituted according to package directions
1	tablespoon	minced fresh garlic (about 4-6 cloves)
1 ½	cups	water or stock (liquid used to soak dried mushrooms works well)
1	tablespoon	naturally-brewed soy sauce or ½ teaspoon sea salt
3	tablespoons	whole wheat flour, spelt or kamut flour
¼	cup	cold water
		salt (or soy sauce) and pepper to taste

Heat oil in a small saucepan over medium heat; add sliced mushrooms and sauté 2-3 minutes. Add garlic, stir well and sauté 1-2 minutes more. Do not let garlic brown. Add water or stock and soy sauce or salt; bring to a boil; reduce heat to low and simmer 5 minutes.

Combine spelt flour and cold water in a small bowl, stirring to blend well. Bring mushrooms and liquid to a boil and add flour-water mixture, stirring continuously until sauce is smooth. Reduce heat to low and simmer 5 minutes, uncovered, stirring occasionally. Adjust seasonings to taste.

Variation: For low-fat version, omit oil or butter and simmer mushrooms and garlic in water or stock. You may also substitute 8 ounces fresh brown or button mushrooms for the fresh shiitakes.

2 cups, or 6 (⅓ cup) portions

*W*hen you begin to live from your Divine Center and to recognize who you Are, you will no longer have any need to be anxious about yourself. Quite spontaneously and perhaps without at first noticing it, now is when you begin to be truly selfless in helping others. You will surprise yourself when you first realize how selfless you have become, but this should not surprise you. You have more energy for them simply because you are no longer consuming the most of it being anxious about yourself!

*Y*ou can make the same mistake working for others that you once made about yourself. Help others come to peace and joy and abundance and health, yes, but never do it on the premise that they are any less secure than you are. This realization will help you work for (and with) others without an overtone of anxiety and tension.

SIMPLE STEAMED VEGETABLES WITH SPICY PEANUT SAUCE

The vegetables in this Indonesian dish are traditionally served chilled and crisp, though they are good warm and more tender, too. The sauce may be varied in spiciness to suit your tolerance for heat. It compliments almost any vegetable; feel free to use what you have on hand. Notice that some here are lightly steamed and others left raw; the degree of cooking is up to you. If you're in a hurry, slice a leftover baked potato and whisk together the sauce ingredients while you steam some frozen veggies; your meal will be ready in minutes!

4-6	small	red potatoes, raw or baked (see An Ovenful of Simple Veggies. p. 44)
2	medium	carrots, trimmed (peeled if desired)
8	ounces	fresh green beans, tough ends and strings removed
¼	head	green cabbage, center core removed
1	bunch	watercress (or 2-3 cups curly endive), washed and trimmed of tough stems
1	batch	Spicy Peanut Sauce (see facing page)
2		hard-boiled eggs, quartered (optional)
¼	cup	purple onion, thin-sliced
½	cup	sliced red radish or diced red bell pepper or vine-ripened tomato
1	small	cucumber, peeled if waxed, sliced in ¼-inch rounds

Wash vegetables. Slice potatoes ¼-inch thick. Cut carrots in half lengthwise, then slice ¼-inch thick across (half-moons) or diagonally. Leave green beans whole or cut diagonally in 2-inch sections. Cut cabbage in ¼-½-inch strips. Set aside potatoes if already cooked; layer raw potatoes and vegetables in a steamer basket placed in a large saucepan or deep skillet. Add water to a level just below the bottom of the basket. Bring to a boil, cover and reduce heat to medium. Steam until potatoes are just tender, about 8-10 minutes. Remove basket and rinse under cold water, or transfer to a colander before cooling. Drain vegetables well. Arrange watercress or endive on individual plates, top with steamed vegetables. Ladle sauce over these; sprinkle onion and radish on top; place two egg wedges on each serving; fan cucumber slices at the base. Yum!

Variation: Serve watercress and steamed veggies on a large platter, with sauce and garnishes in separate bowls on the side. Then let each diner assemble their own creation!

4 servings

*T*here is another silliness you may fall into as you concern yourself more with others. It is good that you wish to share your spiritual peace and joy with them, but that is not to say you are to feel responsible for them. Feeling responsible for others is an ego function. If you listen carefully, you will understand that your Self realizes "others" are not really others at all, and that they already abide in as secure a place as you do—the very same Place.

*O*nly when you experience and respect your-Self as Shared Divine Life can you love yourself securely enough to forget yourself and go serve and love others genuinely. Only then are you secure enough to reach out to others for their own sake as also being Shared Divine Life.

SPICY PEANUT SAUCE

Peanuts can be a source of aflatoxin, a potent carcinogen produced by molds which grow on peanuts, corn and other grain crops which have been weakened or stored improperly. Some producers test their products for the toxin. Ask if yours does.

This sauce is easy to make and keeps up to a week refrigerated. Substitute another nut butter if you don't tolerate peanuts well.

½	cup	natural peanut butter, smooth or crunchy style
2	tablespoons	lemon juice or rice vinegar
1-2	tablespoons	naturally-brewed soy sauce (or salt to taste at end)
1½	teaspoons	minced onion or ½-1 teaspoon minced garlic (optional)
1	tablespoon	concentrated sweetener (apple juice concentrate, maple syrup, honey, etc.)
¼	cup	water or stock
⅛-¼	teaspoon	cayenne pepper or hot sauce to taste

Combine first 5 ingredients in a small mixing bowl. Add water or stock a bit at a time, stirring after each addition, until mixture reaches sauce consistency. Add pepper or hot sauce to taste, but allow a few minutes for flavors to blend before adding too much more.

1 cup

ROASTED FREE-RANGE CHICKEN WITH FRESH HERBS AND GARLIC

"Free-range" means that the bird was actually allowed to move around on the earth to forage for some of its food. They are often also raised without the use of antibiotics, used to treat disease states which are more likely to occur when the chickens are under stress. While they usually cost more than conventionally-grown poultry, buying a whole bird helps makes it economical. If you're cooking for one or two and don't want to eat leftovers 5 days in a row, freeze individual portions for use in quick salads, sandwiches, soups and stews. Roasting is the simplest method of cooking this size chicken. The skin is needed to prevent drying, but it may be removed before eating. If you want even less fat, try cooking a smaller chicken in the slow cooker.

1		3½ - 5 pound roasting chicken
1	tablespoon	each fresh thyme and rosemary, chopped
1-2	tablespoons	minced fresh garlic (about 6-8 large cloves)
1	medium	onion, peeled and quartered
2-3	small	inner stalks of celery, with leaves
2	teaspoons	olive oil

Preheat oven to 450°. Remove giblets and excess fat from the body cavity; rinse the skin and cavity with cold water; place breast side up on a work surface and dry the exterior. Combine the fresh herbs and rub half of them inside the cavity; mix the other half with the minced garlic. Starting at the neck, use your fingers and hand to separate the skin from one side of the breast, then the leg. Repeat on the other side. Spread the garlic and herb mixture evenly under the skin on both sides. Put onion and celery inside the body cavity, then pull skin flaps over the neck and cavity; secure with skewers. Fold wings back and under the body; tie or pin legs together. Rub skin with the oil and place on a rack in a roasting pan. Transfer to the oven and reduce heat to 350°. Bake 25 minutes per pound, or until thickest part of thigh reaches an internal temperature of 185°.

Baste with pan drippings every 15 minutes. Shield breast with a loose tent of foil, if desired; remove foil and untie legs for last 30 minutes of cooking. Allow to rest 15 minutes before carving. Do not leave leftovers at room temperature more than 30 minutes.

Yield: About 6 ounces of boneless, skinless meat for each pound of raw chicken, plus bones for a great chicken stock (see The Resourceful Pot, p. 26).

Quick Variation: Instead of stuffing the herbs and garlic under the skin, place the whole cloves of garlic and sprigs of fresh herbs inside chicken with the onion and celery.

*H*ere is a word of caution about what can cause you not danger, but delay. Never permit your spirituality or meditation to be the subject of small talk. If you chatter on about your inner experiences, you may enjoy everyone's attention for a moment, even their admiration, but you will find you have temporarily diminished and somehow profaned that inner life. Why? Probably because what happens in your spirit is not capable of formulation, much less definition. Except when describing it to your spiritual guide, who knows from experience what is beyond your words, when you try to describe your inner life you are like a child trying to reproduce with crayons the Rembrandt or Van Gogh just seen in a gallery.

SIMPLE BROILED FISH

To cook fish well, first get it fresh. Find a reputable, honest deal... *long its been out of the water, and be sure to smell it before you buy it. Fres... fish has a mild, almost sweet smell, and no trace of "fishyness". Fillets should feel firm and elastic, and have a shiny, moist, translucent look, not dry, milky or discolored. When you get it home, keep it very cold and use it within a day.*

Then cook it simply and don't overcook it. I like what real soy sauce does for just about any fish: natural flavor is enhanced, but not overpowered. A bit of oil helps keep it from drying out. I'm always amazed when people who taste this say it's the best fish they've ever had.

4-6	ounces	fresh fish fillets per person
	light coating	naturally-brewed soy sauce (or lemon juice and a sprinkle of salt)
	juice	from finely-grated ginger (optional)
	a sprinkle of	canola oil or ghee (see p. 70)

Distribute a light coating of soy sauce evenly across surface of fillets with a sanitizable brush or clean fingers. If using ginger, squeeze juice from grated ginger onto surface of fish. Rub surface with oil or ghee. Place on an oiled baking pan or in individual oven-proof serving dishes, folding under the thin tail piece to create a portion of even thickness. Broil or bake for about 10 minutes per inch of thickness. When done, fish will lose all translucency, turning completely opaque, and flake easily with a fork.

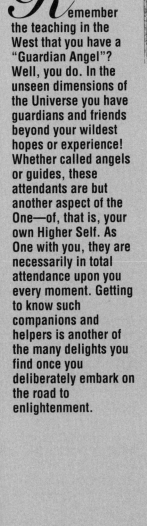

*R*emember the teaching in the West that you have a "Guardian Angel"? Well, you do. In the unseen dimensions of the Universe you have guardians and friends beyond your wildest hopes or experience! Whether called angels or guides, these attendants are but another aspect of the One—of, that is, your own Higher Self. As One with you, they are necessarily in total attendance upon you every moment. Getting to know such companions and helpers is another of the many delights you find once you deliberately embark on the road to enlightenment.

N THE SANCTUARY OF (STUFFED) SOLE

A special dish for a special meal.

2	tablespoons	olive oil or butter
1	small	onion, diced ¼-inch
2	stalks	celery, diced ¼-inch
½	cup	red bell pepper, diced ¼-inch
10	ounces	frozen chopped spinach, thawed and drained
⅓	cup	white wine or ¼ cup water + 2 tablespoons lemon juice
¼	cup	fresh tarragon or dill, chopped
3	cups	whole grain bread cubes
¼	cup	Parmesan cheese, grated, optional
	to taste	salt or naturally-brewed soy sauce and pepper
1½	pounds	fresh sole filets, split in half lengthwise at the natural seam
		soy sauce for dipping filets

Heat oil or butter in a large skillet over medium heat; add onion, celery and bell pepper; sauté, stirring occasionally, about 3 minutes. Add spinach and wine or water; bring liquid just to a boil; reduce heat, cover and simmer 3-5 minutes, or until spinach is just tender. Remove from heat, stir in fresh herbs, add bread and cheese, if used; stir well to blend thoroughly. Add extra liquid if necessary to moisten bread enough to hold together. Allow filling to cool slightly and season to taste. Preheat oven to 375°. Lightly oil a baking tray. Place four mounds of filling on tray, evenly spaced, about 1 cup each. Use hands to create rounded, oblong shapes about 2-inches high. Pour about ¼ cup soy sauce in a large, shallow bowl. Dip one strip of sole briefly into sauce and hold above the bowl to allow any excess to drain off.

Wrap the strip around the sides of a mound of the filling, with the patterned (formerly skin) side facing the filling. Repeat with another strip, overlapping the thinnest ends to create an evenly thick layer of fish. Repeat with all the "sole" you've got until mounds of filling are completely wrapped around the sides, leaving a hole at the top where filling is exposed. Brush top and sides with oil or melted butter.

Bake for 10-12 minutes, until fish has lost its translucency or a wooden pick meets little resistance when pressed into the thickest part. Sprinkle with grated Parmesan and serve immediately with lemon.

4 servings

he words *teacher* and *student*, or the more ancient words *master* and *disciple*, as applied to spiritual studies, have no connotation whatsoever of "have" and "have not." If a teacher acts as though he or she has something the student does not, that master is revealed as having fallen from the path or as having never been on it in the first place. An authentic teacher of spiritual wisdom will start at the very beginning with the premise that every person is equally part of the One. That teacher will immediately remind listening students that they, too, are masters and teachers. All that separates the master from the disciple is a bit of time: one has remembered and one is just beginning to remember.

STIR-FRIED BEEF, VENISON OR BUFFALO WITH GOLD BELL PEPPER AND RED RADISH

Much attention has focused on the ills associated with the high fat, low fiber eating habits of modern western culture. As our understanding of wellness extends beyond the level of personal health, we've begun to see that the food production systems used to support this diet have a significant impact on the environment. Personal as well as planetary health can benefit when resource-intensive, concentrated foods are eaten more occasionally, sparingly, or not at all; habits of many traditional peoples offer wise example of this.

The animals our ancestors used for food were far different than much of what is produced today; the land they inhabited is necessarily limited in this age of increasing population. Happily, some ranchers choose to follow natural, humane methods which are founded in deep respect for life and concern for the integrity of the food they grow as well as the soil and water they steward. Natural beef, venison and even buffalo are being produced with fewer or no chemicals on land otherwise unsuited for food production. It is also now known that domestic animals can be grazed in ways which actually improve certain types of land more than if it were left idle. If you eat meat, use it wisely, as part of a natural, fiber-rich diet. And consider supporting wise resource management. What we do to the earth, we do to ourselves.

In Asian cuisines, ginger and radish are believed to help balance digestion of meats. If you like your steak prepared more simply, broil it to your liking and serve the veggies as a side dish. Have some greens or a salad with it. And know it is blessed by your love.

1	tablespoon	canola oil
1	piece	fresh ginger, 2x1-inch, peeled and minced finely
6	cloves	garlic, minced
1	large	gold bell pepper, cored, seeds removed, sliced thinly
12	ounces	top round or flank steak of natural beef, venison or buffalo, sliced very thinly across the grain
10-12	medium to large	red radishes, trimmed and sliced in thin rounds
	to taste	natural soy sauce or sea salt

Heat oil in a large skillet over medium-high heat. Add ginger, garlic and pepper; sauté until garlic is almost browned. Add meat; sauté until pink is just gone. Add radish; stir well and cook until radish is just heated through. Season to taste. Garnish with roasted sesame seeds if desired.

3-4 servings

SOME MORNINGS FEEL LIKE FRENCH TOAST

One of my earliest cooking memories is of Dad showing us how to make scrambled eggs, French toast or "toads in the hole", that wonderful eggs-cooked-inside-the-bread invention born of the camper's need to do it all in one pan. These days, we're told that because they're high in cholesterol, we should eat the yolks only occasionally; that persons with excessively-high blood cholesterol levels can lower them dramatically by following a diet very low in cholesterol and saturated fat. One would think that the egg, with its digestible, complete protein, would be a wholesome, natural food, well-fit for human consumption. Perhaps it can be, on occasion, for those whose bodies aren't still healing from the habit of fiberless, empty-calorie and high-fat foods.

The amount of egg in one serving of this meal uses up about 1/10 of the fat-gram allotment for an average adult male who wants to keep his fat consumption to 25 percent of total caloric intake (1/6 of a 10% goal). The cholesterol content per serving (about 100 mg.) contributes 1/3 the 300 mg. daily allowance recommended by the American Heart Association. So eat them occasionally, if you do, as part of a diet rich in natural fiber and low in saturated fat. If you must avoid the yolk, replace it with whites, or consider making the eggless version.

2	large	eggs (or 4 ounces firm-style tofu)
1/2	cup	milk, soymilk, water or apple juice
1/4	teaspoon	sea salt
1/2	teaspoon	cinnamon, ground
1/8	teaspoon	nutmeg (optional)
1/2	teaspoon	pure vanilla extract
8	pieces	whole grain bread
		canola oil to lightly coat skillet

Combine eggs with liquid and seasonings, beating lightly with a fork or whisk (for tofu version, puree tofu and liquid until smooth in a blender, then add seasonings and extra liquid if batter is too thick; stir to blend well). Heat oil in a skillet over medium heat; dip bread into batter; allow to soak for 20-30 seconds; shake off excess batter and cook in skillet on each side until golden brown. Serve with Cranberry-Maple Sauce (see p. 81) or Mystic Pear and Apple Topping (see p. 142).

4 servings

S aying that loving yourself is a necessary condition for loving others may seem to be arbitrary and by some pious standards an irreligious statement. Christianity's Founder made love of self the model for loving others: "Love others as you love yourself." Long before organized religion began timidly admitting it, modern psychology had insisted that love and respect for self are needed foundations for all personal and social health.

FRITTATA FOR TWO, EGG OR TOFU

This baked version of an Italian "flat" omelette uses pre-cooked vegetables and an egg or tofu batter to create a hearty meal for two all in one pan. If you use eggs, look for the kind which come from chickens raised in a naturally healthy environment without hormones or antibiotics. Some producers allow them to move freely to forage for some of their food in fresh air and sunlight. To reduce your intake of cholesterol, replace some of the whole egg with whites. The tofu version is cholesterol-free.

1	tablespoon	canola or olive oil
3	eggs	(or 1 whole egg and 4 egg whites), stirred well to blend
		-or-
10	ounces	firm style silken tofu, pureed in a blender until very smooth with ½ cup water or soymilk and ¼ teaspoon sea salt
½	cup	onion, leek or shallot, finely chopped
1½	cups	cooked, well-drained vegetables, chopped
¼	cup	fresh dill (use 2 teaspoons dried), parsley or chives

Preheat oven to 400° for tofu version; 350° for egg version. Lightly oil a 10-inch pie pan. If using eggs, beat lightly in a mixing bowl. Combine remaining ingredients with eggs or pureed tofu in mixing bowl. Spoon mixture into pie pan. Bake for 25-35 minutes, or until batter is set and lightly browned. Cut into 4 wedges before removing from pan; serve two for each serving.

To serve four, double the ingredients; transfer the seasoned, hot vegetables to 2 oiled 9-inch pie tins or one 9x13-inch casserole; bake in the oven until golden brown and set (same time as above for tofu version, about 10-15 minutes for egg version).

sk yourself a simple question each evening: Have I loved myself today in my acts and words and thoughts? Be assured that your progress in the spiritual life is directly proportionate to your honest love for yourself. And what if you have not loved yourself on a given day? What do you do about it? Start again, quite quietly, that very evening and again the next morning. You may be absolutely assured that by the nature of Eternal Reality you will succeed soon enough.

earning to love yourself is not some grand gesture you must learn. It is a small act of kindness or compassion in this moment—now again in this next one—and then yet again in the next. A crippled old cow makes it out of the blizzard and into the barn with one laborious step after another. And, especially if the storm has been fierce, what a gentle and grateful creature she will be when she arrives inside!

EASY SCRAMBLED TOFU WITH VEGETABLES

Here's a nourishing, protein-rich breakfast (or lunch or dinner!) entree free of saturated fat and cholesterol. Tofu's mild flavor lends itself to absorbing those of other foods and seasonings, so experiment with your favorite vegetables, herbs and spices to create a taste you really enjoy. Leftovers make a great egg-salad-like sandwich filling (see p. 119), so consider making a double batch if you're cooking for more than two.

1	tablespoon	vegetable oil
1	bunch	scallions, trimmed of roots and browned leaves, sliced ¼-inch thick with green tops separated from white bottoms
1	small	carrot, trimmed and scrubbed, shredded
¼	teaspoon	turmeric (optional)
1	pound	tofu, drained and crumbled by hand or with potato masher
½	cup	water or stock
		sea salt, to taste
		freshly ground black pepper, to taste

Heat oil in a cast iron or non-stick skillet over medium heat; add white part of scallions and carrot; sauté for about 1 minute, stirring continuously. Add tofu, turmeric and water or stock; stir well.

Bring liquid to a boil; cover and reduce heat to low; simmer for 5 minutes or until liquid is absorbed.

Season to taste. Roasted sunflower or pumpkin seeds complement both the texture and protein of this dish.

Make a double batch and save half for Tofu Salad Sandwiches, (see p. 119).

4 to 6 servings

You are exhibiting significant growth towards enlightenment when you find yourself rising back to joy immediately after any thought, word, act or omission that in a previous day would have distressed or depressed you as a "sin." Quickly, immediately, disregard all thoughts about your "faults," apart from a simple recognition of what it was that went awry of your mark. You are far wiser to give your time and attention to what is eternally right in your Life rather than the inevitable mistakes you make as you are learning to dance.

BROCCOLI BLISS

If you like broccoli, this dish could put you in heaven. If not, salvation may be at hand. You may have heard by now that this vegetable has been shown to contain more than one cancer-preventive substance, but did you know that a 4-inch stalk of broccoli provides about 6-7% of the average daily protein requirement for adult women?

16	ounces	linguini pasta
2	bunches	broccoli
1	cup	Roasted Red Pepper Garnish (make a double batch of recipe on p. 30)
¼	cup	Simple Lemon Vinaigrette (see p. 20) or your favorite vinaigrette-type dressing
¼	cup	pine nuts
¼	cup	grated Parmesan cheese (optional)

Prepare Roasted Red Pepper Garnish (see p. 30); mix with dressing and adjust seasoning to taste.

Cook pasta according to package directions; drain and transfer to covered pasta pot to keep warm.

While pasta cooks, roast pine nuts in a toaster oven at 350° for 5 minutes, or until just beginning to brown; cool. Prepare broccoli: cut to separate lower 3-4 inches of broccoli stems from tender, upper stems and florettes. Peel or slice off tough skin from these; cut in ¼-inch thick diagonal slices as described above. Slice tender upper stems, leaving florettes about 2 inches long. Steam or blanch broccoli and stems until just tender and still bright green. Arrange pasta on serving plates; top with broccoli, then about ⅓ cup sauce for each serving. Garnish with pine nuts and Parmesan cheese if desired.

4 servings

*W*hat is amiss in your life and world is not the presence of something evil in its own right. Darkness is not something in its own right, but only the absence of light. Evil is simply a lack of some due element in a given situation. There is, indeed, pain and injustice in the world, and these are great evils—but "evils" only in the sense that they result from the lack of some due expression of Love, of Eternal Goodness. They are not separately existing "evils," least of all are they the doings of a separately existing evil personage.

SOUTH OF THE BORDER GRILLED TOFU

Versatile tofu joins with Tex-Mex flavors and the convenience of prepared salsa and the calming influence of oregano. This "pizza herb" grows wild in the Mediterranean and Asia.

1	pound	tofu, firm style
1	cup	prepared salsa
1 ½	tablespoons	oregano, fresh (or ¾ teaspoon dried)
1	tablespoon	naturally-brewed soy sauce (optional)
1	tablespoon	extra virgin olive oil or canola oil
1	small	onion, sliced ¼-inch thick
1	small	bell pepper, sliced ¼-inch thick
	as needed	water or stock
2-4	tablespoons	sliced ripe olives
2	tablespoons	fresh cilantro, chopped (optional)

Cut tofu in slices ⅓-inch thick. Combine salsa, oregano and soy sauce, if used, stir well; transfer half of this mixture to a glass or ceramic casserole or dish. Arrange tofu on salsa, then cover with remaining salsa. Allow to marinate at least 2 hours, or as long as 24 hours. Sauté peppers and onions with oil in a non-reactive skillet over medium heat until onions begin to brown. Preheat grill or broiler; lightly oil pan or grill. Brush or wipe off excess salsa from tofu and grill until golden brown. While grilling tofu, add salsa used to marinate tofu to peppers and onions in skillet, stir well and heat until hot, adding extra water or stock as needed to create a sauce consistency. Cut tofu slices diagonally to create triangles if you wish; arrange on plates; top with vegetable-salsa mixture, olives and cilantro, if used.

4 servings

Good Existence is the only kind of Existence there is, and besides this One Existence there is only nothing: no-thing. Apart from what exists, the only conceivable alternate is what is not a thing at all, simply because outside of Existence no-thing exists! Language limps in these realms: if "it" doesn't exist, "it" isn't even there so you can apply the word "it" to it! You will often be amused by this sort of conceptual limping as enlightenment comes to your consciousness, and you find your mind wobbling and your tongue falling all over itself in confusion! Be patient. You will learn to dance without trying to count out the music.

FROM ROME TO BOMBAY (QUICK TOFU CHICKEN OR BEEF CURRY)

Sometimes, you make so much more than you need that you find yourself trying to come up with several different ways to use the same dish. Here's a good example. Zucchini and Garlic Sauce for pasta on Thursday becomes Unexpected Companions (see p. 120) on Saturday. Leftovers remaining Sunday or Monday definitely want to taste different. That's when the spice cabinet comes in handy! Have no leftover sauce? Use a similar quantity of chopped fresh or canned peeled tomatoes; adjust seasonings to taste. This quick meal can be ready in 15 minutes or less.

1	tablespoon	canola oil or ghee
½	small	bell pepper chopped (optional)
8	ounces	firm-style tofu, free-range chicken breast or lean natural beef, diced ½-inch
½ to ¾	cup	Zucchini and Garlic Sauce (see p. 85)
½	teaspoon	cumin, ground
½	teaspoon	mild curry powder
1	tablespoon	grated fresh ginger (trim bad spots, peeling not necessary)
	to taste	sea salt and/or hot sauce or cayenne pepper

Heat oil or ghee in a skillet over medium heat. Add pepper, sauté 30 seconds. Add tofu or meat, stir well and sauté until lightly browned. Add sauce and dry spices; stir well. Using a garlic press or your fingers, squeeze juice from grated ginger into skillet. Moisten dry ginger with water before squeezing again to extract as much juice as possible. Stir well. Bring to a simmer; reduce heat to low and simmer, adding water or stock if desired, for 5 minutes. Adjust seasoning to taste.

2 servings

…BREASTS WITH CHILI-LIME SAUCE

…our heart from too much fat and cholesterol, skinless
…en offer a bit less of these nutrients than the other parts.
They're not exactly a "whole" food, but they are convenient, and lend their
delicate tenderness to special dishes. In this recipe, the marinade becomes a
mildly spicy sauce. If you like yours hot, add cayenne pepper or hot sauce
to taste.

2	tablespoons	olive or canola oil
3	tablespoons	freshly-squeezed lime juice
2	tablespoons	naturally-brewed, reduced sodium soy sauce
4	teaspoons	chili powder
3-4	cloves	garlic, minced
4	(4-6) ounce	free-range chicken breasts, boneless, skinless
½	cup	cool water or stock
1	tablespoon	whole wheat pastry or kamut flour
	to taste	salt or soy sauce and pepper to taste
4-6	sprigs	fresh cilantro for garnish

In a small glass or stainless steel mixing bowl, combine one
tablespoon of the oil with the lime juice, soy sauce, chili
powder and garlic; stir well to blend. Use a sharp knife to trim
any fat off chicken breasts, then score (note: scoring is
optional) the smooth side of each as follows: use the knife to
make shallow cuts ½-inch apart diagonally across the entire
surface, then repeat the cuts at an angle which creates a
diamond pattern across the surface of each. Transfer the
marinade to a glass pie plate or casserole dish, then add the
chicken, turning once to thoroughly coat both sides with the
marinade. Cover and refrigerate; allow to marinate for 1-4
hours, turning once if possible. Drain chicken breasts; reserve
marinade. Heat remaining oil in a large skillet over medium-
high heat. When oil is hot; arrange chicken in skillet, scored
side down. Cook until lightly browned, about 3 minutes, then
turn and repeat on other side. Add reserved marinade to skillet;
bring liquid to a simmer; cover and reduce heat to low. Simmer
6-8 minutes, or until chicken is fork tender and juice runs clear.
Transfer chicken to a serving platter. Combine the water and
flour in a small bowl; stir well to blend, then add to the liquid
in the skillet. Stir continuously over medium heat until liquid
thickens; reduce heat to low and simmer for 3-4 minutes.
Adjust seasonings to taste, then pour sauce over chicken
breasts. Garnish with cilantro.

4 servings

You will do well no longer to imagine that you have to outwit or outmaneuver some evil being existing beside you in this world. When you realize this and gain a confidence in the universal goodness of Reality, your whole view of the universe, of society, of yourself and of your relationship with God will lighten up. You will never dance the dance of the cosmos until you lighten up!

Creative Snacks & Sandwiches

I OPEN MYSELF TO LIFE'S ENERGY BY ALLOWING CONTINUOUS
CHANGE IN MY DIET.

Life reflects continuous change and growth. Cycles of the day, the
month, the seasons, patterns of weather, stages in personal growth,
relationships, all in constant motion, ever-changing unfoldment.
When my diet is repetitive, or static, I deprive my body of the energy
and vitality of change. I am much more adaptive and receptive to the
energy around me when I rotate among the full range of foods of the
earth. My physical needs are unique and continually shift with
changes in activity level, age, mental and emotional needs, as well as
natural and social changes in the environment around me. I can listen
to my body as I experiment with the combinations and proportions of
the foods I eat, and take time for self-reflection to attune to my
constantly-changing needs.

CREATIVE SNACKS AND SANDWICHES

Both these food groups can be convenient as well as healthful. With a willingness to experiment, they also provide an opportunity for creative use of delicious leftovers and high-quality, store-bought prepared foods.

Sandwiches offer nutritional goodness in the form of one of the most ancient of convenience foods - whole grain breads. From the pita and chapati flatbreads of the Middle East and India to the corn tortillas of the New World, traditional breads of the world are available in an incredible variety today. In recent years, conscientious bakers have returned to the simple ways and ingredients of their ancestors.

The few sandwich offerings here only hint at the endless number of possibilities for healthful meals. Wholesome snacks can be a significant source of nutrients for bodies which don't always get what they need in three (or two!) meals. To get the most for your calories, make them count by building healthy snacks around whole grains and legumes or other lean protein sources, and lots of vegetables and fruits. These basic foods have proven satisfying as well as safe for thousands of years.

THE ULTIMATE SNACK

After many years and millions of dollars worth of trial and error testing, sophisticated market research, consumer taste panels and focus groups, the food industry has still not produced a snack food which matches the nutritional quality, convenience, taste, satisfiability and yes, even the "mouthfeel" of what trees have been making for ages. And these ancient beings, in all their wisdom, give back to the soil and the air we breathe at least as much as they take.

1	plum, pear, peach, persimmon, pomegranate, pawpaw, apricot, apple, orange, tangerine, grapefruit, nectarine, fig (or two!) banana, or kiwi (grown with the healthiest soil and as few chemicals as possible)

Wash with cool water. Dry well; place in your fannypack, backpack, briefcase or purse. Take with you wherever you go, especially when the alternative is likely to be food from machines.

Note: For citrus fruits, the small peelers which allow easy removal of the skin, but not the nutritious white part, are indispensable.

---

*S*ome folk see Reality as it actually is, and some as they've attempted to remake it; they see it as they have lied to themselves and perhaps others about it. Even this substantial mistake, however, is no reason to feel guilty or despondent. It is very easy to turn around and see the Light as soon as we know it is there. After all, we don't have far to search for the Light: "The Kingdom of God is within you"—your inner Nature is shared Eternal Being.

SPICY BEAN DIP

This simple dip is great with blue corn tortilla chips. If you're taking a break from corn, try crispy, thin-sliced raw carrots! Their cool sweetness balances the heat. When short on time, use your favorite canned refried beans in place of the homemade version. Then next time you make your own, you might think to freeze enough to have on hand when unexpected guests arrive!

1½	cups	"The Ancient Ones" refried beans, (see p. 67)
		-or-
1	(16-ounce)	can refried beans, lard free, preferably organically-grown
1	cup	your favorite salsa
2	ounces	Cheddar, Monterey Jack cheese or soy cheese, grated
¼	cup	cilantro, chopped (about ¼ -⅙ bunch)

Combine beans and salsa in a saucepan over medium heat. Stir to blend well. Heat until hot. Stir in grated cheese, if used, and cilantro; reduce heat to low and simmer 5 minutes to allow flavors to blend. Serve warm, with cilantro and/or grated cheese garnish.

Yield: about 2½ cups; will vary depending upon the "snack appetite" of the cook!

*O*ne of the most advanced counsels of a past age of spiritual development was the exhortation to "practice the Presence of God." This was great wisdom for that era, but if you analyze the words, they make about as much sense as if someone were to urge you to "practice the presence of your brain." In their frantic concern for conformity and uniformity, those overly institutionalized ages all but forgot the basic message of the persons of high prayer which told us that we are all One with God. They forgot even though this message was clearly stated in an ancient Christian hymn reproduced in Christian scriptures: "In God we live and move and have our Being."

*R*emember the Presence of God? Well, yes, but you will be closer to the point if you remember that right here and right now the Source Being is present and individualizing as yourSelf!

TOFU SALAD FOR SANDWICHES

This can be as simple as adding a bit of your favorite mayonnaise to some leftover Scrambled Tofu. The ingredients offered here result in a somewhat traditional egg salad taste, with the pleasant addition of fresh dill.

1	batch	(4 ½ cups) Scrambled Tofu (see p. 110)
1	large stalk	celery, trimmed and diced ¼-inch
1	medium	carrot, shredded
1	tablespoon	fresh dill weed, chopped (or ½ teaspoon dried)
1	tablespoon	prepared mustard
¼ - ⅓	cup	mayonnaise or Creamy Tofu Dressing (see p. 21)
		salt and pepper to taste

Combine all ingredients in a mixing bowl and stir well to blend. Allow flavors to blend 30 minutes, if possible, before serving.

Variation: Omit vegetables; simply combine Scrambled Tofu and seasonings. If you have no leftover Scrambled Tofu, use crumbled plain tofu; adjust seasonings to taste.

Use your favorite fresh herbs and spices - tofu is happy in the company of any!

see p. 110; see p. 21

---

*H*ere is a point you will gain much from pondering. In reference to yourself, it is not nearly so accurate to use the phrase "God *individualized* as you" as it is to say "God *individualizing* as you." Your origin is not a past event, but an ongoing, instant-by-instant process.

*Y*our only true point of reference is within. It is your very Self, not some Deity out across a boundless universe. Strive to realize early that the Source you seek is not only not "out there"—neither is It "in here." God is neither within nor without. It is the Ultimate Existence that out-presses as all things, including yourSelf. Eternal Existence is expressing Itself as you.

UNEXPECTED COMPANIONS

Irene had the vegetarian version of this surprisingly good open-faced sandwich one night for dinner, several days after Spaghetti with Zucchini-Garlic Sauce. I wanted chicken. Ah, the blessings of leftovers. Yes, avocados are high in fat (30 grams each), but it is high-quality, unrefined, unprocessed fat, mostly of the monounsaturated variety. The chicken version contains about 20 grams of fat, which adds up to about 36 percent of the total number of daily fat grams allowed for a healthy adult male's 25 percent-of-calories-from-fat-type diet. Since the bulk of my diet comes from low-fat, fiber-rich vegetable sources, I had plenty of room for this joyful feast.

4	slices	whole grain bread, preferably natural sourdough
1	ripe	avocado
2	ounces	skinless, sliced Roasted Free-Range Chicken (see p. 104) (optional)
½	cup	Zucchini-Garlic Sauce (see p. 85)
	to taste	thinly-sliced purple onion

Toast the bread. Mash the avocado on the bread. Put the chicken on two of the pieces of bread, on top of the avocado. Spread 2 tablespoons of the sauce on the avocado of the two meatless pieces; use the same amount on the chicken. Top with onion, if desired. Enjoy your meal, and appreciate your differences.

Variation: Substitute your favorite cheese for the chicken; use any good, thick tomato sauce if you have no Zucchini-Garlic Sauce.

2 servings

I s it difficult for you to be told that you are an out-pressing of Eternal Being, Eternal Life? Look closely and you will realize that it is not difficult but just different from what you have always heard and probably been taught. Actually, if you have courage enough to consider it honestly, it makes more sense to see the Eternal Being as out-pressing as all things than to think of It in the older stories where our Source is a distant potter or clock maker in the skies.

SLOPPY JOES OR TOFU JACKS

Over 1,000 years ago, the Chinese discovered that freezing tofu in the snow enhanced its texture and ability to absorb other flavors. This process also made for good fuel economy by reducing the need to prepare fresh batches more often. Their thriftiness, born of a close relationship with limited resources, can benefit us today: the lower cost of tofu reflects the fact that it requires much less of both living and fossil fuel energy to produce than a similar quantity of animal protein. Whichever you choose, enjoy a childhood memory.

2	tablespoons	olive or canola oil
2	medium	onions, chopped
2	medium	bell pepper, chopped
4	cloves	garlic, minced
1	pound	ground, skinless natural chicken or turkey or extra lean natural beef -or-
1	pound	tofu, firm style
3	medium	vine-ripened tomatoes, peeled (see p. 35) and chopped, with liquid
1	(16-ounce)	can tomato sauce
1	tablespoon	chili powder
¼	cup	chili sauce, barbeque sauce or ketchup

For Tofu Jacks, slice tofu about ⅓-inch thick; arrange slices on a lightly oiled plate and freeze for at least 12 hours; texture improves with lengthier freezing up to several months (if freezing extra for later use, transfer frozen slices to a sealed plastic bag). Before use, thaw tofu in a bowl of very hot or boiling water, then remove and press gently to expel as much water as possible; crumble or chop each slice into ¼-inch chunks. Heat oil in a large skillet over medium-high heat. Add onion and bell pepper; sauté until onion begins to brown. Reduce heat to medium and add ground meat or tofu. Stir often for poultry or meat version; cook until meat loses its pink color. Add remaining ingredients, stir well, then reduce heat to low and simmer 15 minutes. Serve on whole grain burger buns.

Quick Variation: Substitute 1 (16-ounce) can whole, peeled tomatoes for the fresh ones.

For reduced fat content with ground beef, brown it in a dry skillet, then drain fat before adding onions and peppers.

about 7 cups; freezes well

BONZO BEAN SPREAD

A roommate of mine had a dog named Bonzo whose irritating skin condition and poor vision healed completely when we fed him whole grains, legumes and vegetables. His disposition improved, too.

This spread is a variation on "Hummus bi Tahini" - the famous chickpea dip from the Middle East. Served there for centuries, it makes efficient use of the complementary proteins of beans and seeds. Tahini is a "butter" made from ground, hulled, sesame seeds. This version is a bit thicker than the traditional dip. Use it with lettuce, tomato and sprouts on a sandwich, or as an appetizer spread with crackers. Thin it with more olive oil or bean cooking liquid if you'd like a dip for pita or vegetables.

2	cups	well cooked (but not to the "gravy" stage) Garbanzo Beans, drained
¼	cup	lemon juice
¼	cup	tahini
2	tablespoons	fresh thyme leaves (or ½ teaspoon dried)
¼	teaspoon	freshly-ground black pepper
½	teaspoon	sea salt, or to taste
2	tablespoons	purple onion, finely chopped
¼	cup	red bell pepper, finely chopped
1-2	tablespoons	freshly-grated horseradish (optional)
2-4	tablespoons	extra virgin olive oil or bean-cooking liquid to thin to desired texture

Combine the first six ingredients in a food processor and blend until smooth.

Note: Most blenders will not puree such a thick mixture, so if you don't have a food processor, mash beans in a mixing bowl, using a fork, potato masher or whisk (or use a manual food mill), then stir in lemon and whisk until smooth before adding remaining ingredients and stirring well to mix thoroughly.

Add minced onion, pepper and horseradish; stir well to blend. Add oil or bean liquid as desired.

You may use the processor to mince the onions and peppers, but remove them before pureeing the other ingredients, then stir them into the finished puree; otherwise, they'll puree too, and you'll lose some of the texture and distinctive color contrast created by the individual bits of vegetable. Or maybe you *want a pink dip…*

Variation: Try ¼ cup chopped parsley instead of thyme; use 2-3 teaspoons minced garlic instead of onion.

2½- 3 cups

Your understanding of love, however, does change in the sense that the word love implies an I and a Thou, one who loves and one who is loved. But what happens to this duality when both lover and beloved are seen to be One? Then we must more accurately speak of Union. When love turns into conscious Union, it becomes a dance. Dance is truly all the soul can do at those times when Union presses it.

All the way to realized union with the Eternal is union already. Understand that and you will break out dancing.

"TLT" WITH SESAME "BACON"

A cooking class student once served these to some friends who don't care for tofu. She got raves.

The key to getting the bacon flavor is to roast the sesame condiment a bit longer than usual, until a bit darker than light brown. The key to convenience is having extra condiment on hand from a good-sized batch made previously. Tender, moist whole-grain bread and fresh, vine-ripened tomatoes add the finishing touches.

1	pound	tofu, firm-style, drained
¼	cup	naturally-brewed soy sauce for dipping tofu
1	tablespoon	sesame oil
8	slices	whole-grain bread
½	cup	Creamy Tofu Dressing (see p. 21) or your favorite mayonnaise
½	cup	Roasted Sesame Condiment (see p. 124)
4	leaves	greenleaf lettuce
8	slices	ripe tomato

Cut the tofu into 10 slices of equal thickness. Lay across half of a doubled towel, then fold other half over top of tofu and press gently to squeeze out excess water. Pour the soy sauce into a shallow-sided container. Dip each tofu slice into soy sauce, shake off excess sauce, transferring tofu to a plate. Heat oil in a large cast iron or non-stick skillet over medium heat. When hot, place tofu slices in skillet and pan-fry until light brown, about 3-5 minutes on each side.

While tofu is browning, toast bread lightly. Spread one side of each slice with 1 tablespoon of dressing. Sprinkle 1 tablespoon of sesame condiment evenly over each; arrange 2 tofu slices on each of 4 slices of the dressed toast, then tomato slices, lettuce and other dressed toast slice. Serve while warm.

4 servings

ROASTED SESAME CONDIMENT

This Japanese condiment has a bacon-like flavor, especially if the seeds are roasted until well-browned. The traditional way to grind the seeds is with a ceramic grinding bowl, or suribachi, using a wooden pestle-like utensil called a surikogi. A blender or food processor will do, but the hand-grinding method is peaceful and rhythmic, reason enough to have a suribachi on hand (available at Oriental markets and natural food stores). The gentle saltiness of this condiment makes it a great companion for simply-cooked grains or veggies. Use less salt if you like, or substitute a toasted sea vegetable, which adds extra high-quality calcium and many trace minerals, or use the roasted seeds as is to garnish vegetables, grains and stir-fry vegetables. Refrigerate or freeze whatever you won't use soon.

1	cup	unhulled sesame seeds
1 ½	teaspoons	sea salt

Rinse seeds briefly under cold running water in a fine - mesh strainer; drain well. Heat a heavy-bottomed stainless steel or cast-iron skillet over medium-high heat. Add seeds to hot skillet; stir continuously until seeds are dry and begin to pop, about 3-5 minutes. Reduce heat to medium and continue to stir until seeds are golden brown, about 3-5 more minutes. Combine warm seeds and salt in a suribachi, blender or food processor and grind (or pulse, if electric) until most seeds are coarsely ground.

Sesame-Sea Vegetable Condiment: Roast 1-2 ounces of wakame or sea palm fronds on a baking pan in a 300° oven for about 10 minutes. Wakame should be crispy and dry when it cools. While wakame is roasting, prepare and roast the seeds as described above. When wakame is cool, pulverize it in the implement of your choice; sift out any coarse stem pieces, then add the warm sesame seeds and grind as above. Adjust saltiness to taste with sea salt.

about 1 cup

*E*veryone will inevitably come to a full realization of who and what they Are, that is, to heaven, but many unnecessarily suffer hell in the meantime as they try to plow with their vacuum.

ALMOND-MISO SPREAD

This savory spread is versatile-use it on crisp rye crackers, wholegrain toast or crisp, raw slices of spicy daikon radish. "Miso", a traditional Japanese seasoning, is made by fermenting soybeans, grain and sea salt. It is relatively salty, but provides a richness of flavor far beyond the 5 - 13% sodium it contains. Japan National Cancer Institute studies have shown a correlation between miso consumption and lower rates of some forms of cancer. The natural enzymes and bacteria it contains enhance digestion in a manner not unlike yogurt, and because it contains an abundance of the amino acids commonly deficient in grains, miso acts as a protein booster, enhancing the protein quality of these foods. Misos which are lighter in color and sweeter in taste have been aged for as few as 6 months, versus up to three years for the darker, saltier varieties.

½	cup	almond butter
2	tablespoons	miso
1	tablespoon	lemon juice
2	tablespoons	wild onions, minced
		-or-
1	clove	garlic, minced
2	tablespoons	fresh parsley, chopped
3	tablespoons	water, or more, depending on texture desired

Combine first five ingredients in a small mixing bowl; stir to blend well. Add water slowly while stirring; use more if necessary to get desired consistency. Allow flavors to blend at least an hour before serving.

Variation: For a lighter colored spread, replace the almond butter with tahini. If miso is unavailable, use sea salt or naturally-brewed soy sauce to taste before adding water to adjust texture.

about 1 cup

SPICED ROASTED PEPITAS AND SUNFLOWER SEEDS

When I want a snack, I often think "crunch." And sometimes, when I want "crunch", I want oil as well. Or at least, that's what my body seems to say. And why not? Consuming a diet rich in whole grains, legumes, vegetables and fruits, with small amounts of animal protein, I get far less fat than those eating a standard American diet. Some fats have been called "essential" because they cannot be synthesized by our bodies. They must come from our diet. And what better way to get it than straight from the foods nature provides? Doesn't that make more sense than extracting the oil from natural sources and processing the heck out of it, just so we can heat it to damaging temperatures and dip otherwise lowfat foods into it?

This mixture of seeds is great with a raw vegetable snack, and also adds texture and flavor to simple grain dishes. Pumpkin seeds are a fair source of omega-3 fatty acids, which have been shown to lower blood cholesterol and triglyceride levels, thus inhibiting hardening of the arteries.

1	tablespoon	water
¼	teaspoon	sea salt
¾	teaspoon	cumin, ground
¾	teaspoon	chili powder
¾	cup	raw pumpkin seeds
¾	cup	raw sunflower seeds

In a small bowl, combine the water, salt and spices; stir to dissolve and allow to soak while roasting the seeds. Dry-roast the seeds in a cast-iron or stainless steel skillet over medium heat, stirring continuously until sunflower seeds turn light brown and pumpkin seeds have "puffed" from flat to a rounded shape. Stir the spice-water mixture once more before sprinkling into the skillet with the seeds; stir quickly to coat the seeds evenly. Continue to roast until seeds are dry. Allow to cool before serving.

1 ½ cups

A little child is cared for regardless of how improvident and careless he or she may be. Eventually, however, a child is expected to grow up and care for itself. It is much the same in the inner life. When we have grown a certain degree and are beginning to attain a higher awareness, the time arrives when if we want health and abundance it becomes *our* responsibility to be healthy and abundant. We have been told in many sacred writings that "As we believe, so is it done for us."

THE WILD ONE

Foods which grow without human assistance were available long before cultivation began. They have survived naturally, adapting themselves to the unique conditions of their local environment, unhampered by considerations such as how large or shipping-tolerant they might become. Flourishing with incredible diversity, often despite our concrete and asphalt barriers, these edibles have persisted with vitality and natural beauty unmatched by any of their well-bred modern cousins. Perhaps it is this elemental strength and vigor which manifests such potent nutritional value. The lambsquarters mentioned on page 51 contain as much as twice the vitamin A as commonly cultivated greens; the curly dock, purslane and common wild violet leaves which grow in my neighborhood contain from 2 to 6 times the vitamin C of oranges. These differences may only hint at benefits which are still immeasurable. It is possible to feel them, though.

This recipe is based on edibles available in many parts of Eastern and Central North America; those who live elsewhere may derive similar satisfaction from an assortment of bitter, pungent and sour tastes offered by the wild ones in their locale. Learn to positively identify wild edibles of your area. Let some of them grow in your garden or flower beds. Then take a snack like this on an empty stomach some spring afternoon.

1-2		wild onions or garlic, green part
small	handful	young spring cress, Pennsylvania Bittercress or peppergrass
	a pinch of	common sorrel or wood sorrel
	a few leaves	young dandelion or wild mustard
	a few	sunflower seeds or almonds, raw

Pick only enough for a small handful. Wash under cool water. Add a dash of salt if desired. Don't bother with a bowl or plate, these were the first "fingerfoods" ever invented. Chew well.

Yield: Potent nourishment; greater appreciation for earthly gifts.

WHEN YOU NEED NO SNACK

I'm in between a meal, or late at night, and wonder what to eat, I'd like a bite...of what? Maybe some chips or sweet, cold white stuff - no, I watch my health, I need the right stuff: a piece of fruit or veg or ricecake; I want some popcorn, quick 'n easy micro-bake. Some kind of liquid - sweet, refreshing...or maybe hot and stim-u-lating. If only I can choose the perfect food now, I think my life today will be WOW! Might start to look like them on TV, won't have to feel, except what's easy. Taste...eat...ENJOY!

Food (food), n. 1. any nourishing substance that is eaten or otherwise taken into the body to sustain life , provide energy, promote growth, etc....

Appreciation for the balancing effects of natural eating habits sometimes leads me to focus on food as the solution to my problems. Because daily food choices strongly influence my health, this is an important area to examine. But if the dictionary definition is taken literally, should I not consider the air and water I consume to be food, as well? And what of the nourishment offered by sunlight? Or the comforting touch of a caring friend? Yes, physical sustenance involves much more than foods of the earth. At times, my ability to receive balanced nourishment is enhanced by rest from eating. Our digestive systems benefit from rest. Pure water can allow that. If it's sweetened, even with a non-caloric substance, what might be the message my body is receiving? What does this miraculously intricate combination of cells and synapses do to respond to a taste which naturally would come along with other nutrients and complex carbohydrates? Do we really know?

After a lifetime of better-tasting, new-and-improved, it may take a while to adjust to the natural liquid of nature. Try this beverage, which is said to have a mild cleansing and tonifying effect on the liver. I've found it does wonders for the symptoms of a cold. Try it in the morning as soon as you arise, at least ½ hour before eating.

1	cup	pure water
¼		lemon

Heat the water until just warm, then squeeze the lemon juice into it. Drink while warm. Breathe deeply. Talk to a friend.

You may find yourself wondering or complaining at times about why you suffer so much or have so many unfilled needs when it seems to you that you are doing everything you can on the spiritual path. "Why isn't God answering my pleas as formerly?" Well, perhaps you are doing all you can, and maybe there is nothing more you should be doing. Instead of doubting yourself and moping about in guilt as to how you must be somehow failing, consider that perhaps you are *not* failing! Maybe what is being quietly suggested to you is, "Friend, come up higher!" Maybe you are being invited to new realms of self-actualization and self-realization.

APPLE-LEMON COOLER

And then there are times when you WANT it sweet, cold and refreshing, as well. This drink provides the thirst-quenching effect of lemonade without super-refined or artificial sweeteners. Even apple juice is a concentrated source of sugar without the naturally-occurring fiber which helps our bodies use it. Diluting it a bit makes sense, especially for those who don't tolerate sugar well. Omit the water if you like; the lemon still helps to balance the sweetness.

1	quart	organic apple juice
2	cups	water, or the equivalent volume of ice cubes
¼-⅓	cup	freshly-squeezed lemon juice, to taste

Combine all ingredients and chill.

6 servings

SUMMER SMOOTHIE

Fruit-sweet, quick and easy, this shake-like beverage will cool you down in a hurry while it nourishes your body. Use this recipe as a guide to create your own special blend using other juices and fruits.

1		banana
1	cup	(5 ounces) frozen strawberries
1	cup	apple or apple-strawberry juice

Combine fruits and juice in a blender and puree until smooth. Enjoy the fruits of your labor.

PINE-APPLE TEA

Almost 400 years before ascorbic acid (vitamin C) was chemically identified and isolated, natives of the area near present-day Montreal showed the French explorer Cartier how to cure scurvy with a tea made using twigs and needles of White Pine or Eastern Hemlock. They are also rich in beta-carotenes which offers natural protection against certain types of cancer.

Light green needles from new spring growth make the best tea, but older needles may be used as well.

I like the sweetness provided by apple juice, but the unsweetened beverage is good, too.

½	cup	finely-chopped pine needles and tender twig tips
1	cup	unfiltered, organic apple juice (optional)
1	cup	pure water

Combine all ingredients in a small glass or stainless steel pot and bring just to a simmer over medium heat. Reduce heat to very low and allow to steep, barely simmering, about 15 minutes.

*W*hat does it mean to say that it is ultimately up to you to "manifest" the happiness and health and abundance you want? You will find it helpful if you try to understand this clearly and not just feel obliged to blindly believe it. There is only one Life in the Universe, and that Life is that of the Eternal Source, infinite and in no way divisible. (After all, how could Existence be limited or divided?) If you share that Existence—and you do or you would not be here—you have It completely, for, again, it is not divisible. You are part and parcel of all the riches of Its Out-pressings throughout all Reality. Go ahead, then! Kick up your heels! *Create* the fulfillment of all your needs *and* wants! Image whatever pertains to your well-being and that of your loved ones and your world and, believing What you Are, watch it all come true!

Desserts

FOODS OF THE EARTH ARE GIFTS OF LIFE, OFFERING VITALITY, STRENGTH AND SUPPORT ON MY PATH OF SERVICE. I ENHANCE THEIR NUTRITIOUS AND HEALING EFFECTS WHEN I RECEIVE THEM WITH GRATITUDE AND FAITH.

There are times when I see the labor of food preparation as a chore of drudgery, to be finished as soon as possible to get on with the "real" business of life. With that perspective, I am better off dining at a good restaurant or eating lovingly-prepared convenience foods. The difference in my health is noticeable, however, when I choose to participate with gratitude in the selection of my meals. Perhaps it's the physical contact with the colors and shapes of the fresh ingredients, or the fact that I'm more likely to prepare foods which just aren't available elsewhere. Maybe it's the blessing I bestow upon this daily bread with my lightened heart.

I can take time for a quiet moment of thanks and affirmation of the Love embodied in the fruits of earth's labor. It need not be complex or conventional to have creative power:

I give thanks for these gifts
and see them as blessed, full of loving nourishment
for my body
that I may better be of service to myself and others.

As I choose foods which bring balance and nourishment to myself, I support the health of earth as well, helping to free resources to be used in more efficient ways and to nourish others.

DESSERTS

As I've gained an appreciation for the simple sweetness of wh: vegetables and fresh fruits, the desire for concentrated sweeten: diminished greatly. Desserts, once eaten at the end of every m... ... now more likely to be consumed on special occasions or just for fun.

Commonly associated with sugar and fat, these foods need not contribute lots of empty calories to our diet. Whole grain flours, fruits and fruit juices, nuts and seeds and mellow sweeteners can help desserts become a source of fiber-rich, complex carbohydrates as well as protein, vitamins and minerals. Many people find they tolerate some of the more "complex" sweeteners, such as barley malt syrup and brown rice syrup, much better than simpler sugars. If you'd like to try these liquid sweeteners in your favorite recipes, substitute equal amounts of syrup for honey or maple syrup; if replacing dry sweeteners such as sugar and fructose, reduce liquid ingredients by ⅓. Keep in mind, though, that malt syrups can inhibit the thickening effect of natural starches such as arrowroot and kudzu.

CRISPY BROWN RICE BARS

These no-bake treats are reminiscent of a childhood favorite made with refined grain and sweeteners. This version offers more nourishment as well as that unique crispy-crunch!

¼	cup	almond or peanut butter
⅓	cup	brown rice syrup (or ¼ cup honey)
½	cup	chopped, roasted almonds or peanuts (optional)
½	cup	currants
½	teaspoon	vanilla extract
½	teaspoon	cinnamon, ground
4	cups	crispy brown rice cereal

Combine all but the cereal in a mixing bowl; stir to blend well. Add cereal and stir gently until well-mixed. With moistened hands, press evenly into a lightly-oiled 8x12-inch rectangular baking pan or casserole dish.

Chill for at least 1 hour. Cut into 24 pieces.

ᴀNANA-BERRY DREAMS

Kanten is the Japanese word for agar, a sea vegetable used to make gelatin-like desserts. It is easily digested, virtually fat-free, non-caloric and contains significant amounts of calcium and magnesium.

4	cups	apple-raspberry or apple-strawberry juice, or cranberry-juice blend
6	tablespoons	kanten or agar flakes
2	tablespoons	juice concentrate, maple syrup or honey (optional)
2	tablespoons	arrowroot, kudzu or cornstarch
3	cups	fresh raspberries, strawberries or blueberries
4	small	bananas, organically-grown (or use 3 large)

If using strawberries, remove stems and cut in half. Measure 3½ cups of the juice into a saucepan; sprinkle the agar flakes on the juice; bring to a simmer over medium heat without stirring. Simmer, stirring occasionally, 2-3 minutes. Stir starch into remaining juice; stir well to dissolve, then stir into simmering juice-agar mixture; continue to stir until mixture returns to a simmer and is thickened and clear. Remove from heat; add berries to hot liquid. Partly immerse hot pan in a sink of cool water, stirring occasionally for about 2-3 minutes to cool slightly. Slice bananas; divide berries and bananas between two 9-inch pie plates (or place all in the bottom of a 1½-quart glass bowl). Pour juice-agar blend over fruit. Refrigerate or set in a cool place, covered, until set, about 1-2 hours. Serve garnished with soaked or roasted nuts or yogurt. To invert dessert onto a serving platter, warm bottom of pie plate or bowl briefly in a sink with warm water, then use a rubber spatula to loosen edges of dessert from container. Hold platter on top of plate or bowl; invert and gently tap both on counter until dessert loosens onto platter.

Variation: Distribute fruit and kanten among 6 or 8 individual glass serving bowls or glasses.

Reduce quantities by half if smaller batch desired.

8 servings

*Y*ou can never remind yourself often enough that you are invited, right now, to pure joy. Right now, because, in literal fact ultimate and perfect Joy is right now, with metaphysical necessity, already with you. "With" you? No, It *is* You! Does this seem surprising ? If you had not yet realized it, would it be surprising if you were invited "right now" to recognize that you *already* have a heart and mind? Would you envision a long and laborious process to recognize them?

COCOA-MOCHA MAPLE CAKE

Light on the saturated fat and cholesterol, this treat may help soften a heart in more than one way: try repeating its name 3 times quickly without smiling! For those allergic to chocolate, carob provides a suitable alternative. Also known as "St-John's-Bread", this mineral-rich and naturally sweet powder comes from the bean pod of the Mediterranean Honey Locust tree, and was said to have been eaten in the wilderness by John the Baptist.

My friend Brad suggested the cinnamon to enhance the chocolatey taste.

1	cup	soy, almond or lowfat cow's milk
2	tablespoons	instant de-caffeinated coffee (or instant roasted grain beverage)
1 3/4	cup	maple syrup (or rice or barley syrup plus 1/2 teaspoon maple extract)
1/2	cup	canola oil
1	tablespoon	vanilla extract
1	teaspoon	natural maple extract
3/4	cup	unsweetened cocoa or roasted carob powder
2	cups	whole wheat pastry flour
1/2	cup	unbleached white flour
2	tablespoons	non-aluminum baking powder
3/4	teaspoon	cinnamon, ground
1/4	teaspoon	nutmeg, ground

Preheat oven to 350°. Lightly oil the bottom only of two 9 x 1 1/2-inch round or one 9 x 13 x 1 1/2-inch cake pans. In a large bowl, combine milk and instant coffee; stir until coffee is dissolved. Add maple syrup, oil and extracts; stir well.

Into a separate mixing bowl, sift cocoa or carob powder, using a strainer to remove any lumps. Add other dry ingredients (sift baking powder if lumpy) and stir well with a whisk to mix thoroughly. Add dry mix to liquid and stir with a whisk until batter is smooth. Distribute batter evenly between pans; bake for 25-30 minutes or until an inserted wooden skewer or pick comes out clean. Cool the cake in the pan on a cooling rack until heat is gone. Use a spatula or knife to loosen any edges of cake sticking to the pan; place a clean towel, then another cooling rack on the cake and turn over to drop cake out. Turn cake right side up onto another rack. Brush crumbs from edges before frosting. Store unfrosted cake in an airtight container to keep moist.

16 servings

As joy begins to take over in your life, you may be among the last to know. On a superficial level, in immediate consciousness and work habits, you may continue to feel pressured, rushed and, apart from your time of meditation, as harried as ever. Ego habits do linger! Meanwhile, inside and preconsciously, you are already deeply and honestly aware of spiritual priorities. Your Divine Self patiently tells you there that everything is a game and not at all unsafe. Soon enough, if you don't turn aside in fear or weariness, what is preconscious will break into your conscious mind and you will be caught dancing.

COCOA (OR CAROB) MOCHA FROSTING

Frosting the cake and licking the bowl was an honor granted by a mom who appreciated interest in the kitchen. All little ones should be so lucky.

This spread relies upon wheat starch instead of butter and powdered sugar for creaminess. Whole wheat pastry flour comes from a soft wheat with a low gluten content. Because it is a whole grain flour, the bran is included, sifting it out creates a smoother texture.

2½	cups	soy, almond or lowfat dairy milk
¾	cup	unbleached wite flour (or whole wheat pastry flour, sifted to remove the bran)
3	tablespoons	canola oil
¼	cup	cocoa
¾	cup	maple syrup (or honey and ½ teaspoon maple extract)
2	teaspoons	instant decaffeinated coffee or instant roasted grain beverage
1	teaspoon	pure vanilla extract
½	teaspoon	natural maple extract

Combine 1 cup of the milk with the flour in a measuring cup or small bowl and stir until very smooth and no lumps remain. Combine remaining milk with oil, cocoa, sweetener and instant coffee in a medium saucepan. Stir well with a whisk; bring to a simmer over medium-high heat, stirring frequently. Stir flour and milk mixture well before adding slowly to the saucepan; stir continuously while adding and until mixture is thickened and smooth. Reduce heat to low and simmer 5 minutes, stirring occasionally. Remove from heat; stir in vanilla and maple extract. When frosting is almost completely cool, add a bit of extra milk or sweetener if necessary to thin to spreadable consistency.

Variation: For carob version, replace cocoa with carob and reduce sweetener to ½ cup. Follow directions above, but after bringing carob mixture to a simmer, reduce heat to low and simmer for 5 minutes. Then raise heat to medium-high again before proceeding to stir flour mixture into saucepan.

2½ to 3 cups, depending on how much the pot-licker requires (enough for top and sides of a 2-layer Cocoa-Mocha Cake).

*A*s your enlightenment continues, you begin to suspect and then to realize that nearly all of those things your busyness thinks need doing do not really deserve so much importance—at least not on your ego's schedule. You find yourself apparently distraught, yet somehow deeply at peace. Do you know what to do about this strange state of affairs? Laugh uproariously at yourself—but with a laughter of amused love, not of ridicule or threat.

SPICED FRUIT COMPOTE WITH ROASTED PECANS

For the sweet tooth, dried fruit offers a very nutritious alternative with lots of fiber. If several varieties are soaked and simmered together, the sweetness and laxative effect is mellowed to a gentle, warming and relaxing blend. Stirring a bit after the fruit is tender helps create a sauce. The apricots add a nice tartness to this mixture; try your favorite fruits and spices to create your own heirloom recipe. Then pass it on to someone.

½	cup	apricots, dried
½	cup	peaches, dried
½	cup	apples, dried
½	cup	currants or raisins
3½	cups	water or apple juice
1	stick	cinnamon
1½-inch	piece	fresh ginger, peeled and cut ⅛-inch thick
½	cup	pecan halves

Combine fruit, cinnamon sticks and water in a glass or stainless steel bowl or pot; soak for 6 - 12 hours. Bring to a boil; reduce heat to low and add sliced ginger. Cover and simmer for 30 minutes; stir well, then allow to simmer 15 more minutes. If possible, allow fruit to steep in liquid for 1 hour before serving. To roast pecans, place in a toaster oven at 300° for 5-10 minutes until fragrant and lightly browned. Serve compote hot or chilled, topped with chopped roasted nuts or seeds, granola, or yogurt. (Or whipped cream!) Also makes a great topping for hot cereals - the liquid is a delicious sweetener!

Variation: Substitute or add other whole spices, such as cardamom pods, coriander seeds, fennel seeds and star anise; wrap these in cheesecloth, tie with a string and simmer with fruit; remove before serving.

4-6 servings

*T*here is a rapid and close-at-hand cure for any kind of disturbance you may ever feel. Letting any person, thing or circumstance bother you, is to permit yourself to be kept in a small, dark box. Peer out from under the lid! Ask your angels and guides to help you learn to be light-hearted. Find reassurance in the realization that they are laughing with you. Ask them to help you move to a new level of understanding of the simple adventure of it all. *Consciously* see the clouds, hear the wind, greet the trees, walk on the grass, pat the dog, pet the cat. You are part of all these! Your Life and their Life are facets of the same Life. Listen to everything! Communicate with everything!

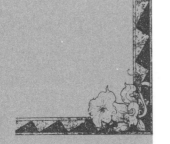

CARDAMOM FRUIT PUDDING

Save some fruit compote next time you make it. This flavorful, soothing pudding is worth having some on hand. The menthol-like flavor of cardamom seeds is very compatible with fruit, and most aromatic when freshly-ground. The whole pods, often used in Indian rice dishes, are green and more flavorful when unbleached. To grind, remove black seeds from 5 or 6 pods, then grind finely with a mortar and pestle.

⅔	cup	fruit juice or liquid from Spiced Fruit Compote (see p.137)
⅓	cup	rolled oats
¼	teaspoon	freshly-ground cardamom
1-2	tablespoons	ghee (see p. 70) (optional)
2	cups (packed)	well-drained fruit from Spiced Fruit Compote
1-2	tablespoons	concentrated sweetener (optional)
1½	teaspoons	pure vanilla extract

Combine juice, oats and cardamom in a small saucepan; bring to a boil, stir well, reduce heat to very low and simmer, covered, for 15 minutes. Stir well, adding ghee, if used; cover and allow to stand 10 more minutes. Measure fruit, optional sweetener and vanilla extract into blender or food processor. Add warm oat mixture and blend until very smooth; turn blender off occasionally and use a rubber spatula to push any pudding on sides to the bottom. When completely smooth, pour pudding into 4-6 serving dishes and chill. Garnish with soaked almonds or filberts or yogurt.

4-6 servings

*G*ive everything around you a chance to teach you about joy. Properly recognized, your surroundings will get you out of your self-maintained crypt of sorrow and fear. At first this sort of guidance may sound naive, like Pollyanna—until you try it and find it works! Meditation is therapeutic because it causes you to remember Reality, even the Reality of the pebble you scuff underfoot. A pebble can make you laugh for joy.

MULBERRY SHORTCAKE

Two of my best friends in our neighborhood are a mature mulberry tree overhanging a fence down the street and the squirrel or bird that planted some of its seed in my yard. The early-summer fruit looks like a small blackberry, but some are seedless and the best varieties are sweet. Even the tender young shoots are said to make a delicious cooked vegetable. If you find a tree with red or black fruit, the ripest, sweetest berries will be easily shaken off the branches or may be pulled with no resistance (and also leave a wonderful color on your hands). If mulberries are not available in your neighborhood, raspberries or blackberries may be substituted.

This recipe uses a whole grain version of "drop biscuits", which may be baked on a cookie sheet or in muffin tins, rather than rolled and cut, which saves a bit of time and mess.

1	cup	whole wheat pastry flour
1	cup	unbleached white or kamut flour (see p. 89)
1	tablespoon	non-aluminum baking powder
½	teaspoon	sea salt
¼	cup	canola oil
1	cup	unfiltered, organic apple juice, room temperature
1	tablespoon	concentrated sweetener (optional)
1	teaspoon	vanilla extract
1	batch	mulberry sauce (see Dancing Hearts Strawberry Sauce, next page)

Preheat oven to 400°; lightly oil a cookie sheet or muffin tin (or use paper cups in tin). Combine dry ingredients in a mixing bowl and stir well to mix thoroughly. In a separate bowl, whisk together liquid ingredients. Add liquid ingredients to dry mix and stir briefly to just moisten dry ingredients - no more than 10 to 20 seconds of gentle mixing, or biscuits will be tough (it's not necessary to smooth out every small lump). Drop ¼-cup portions of batter onto cookie sheet or into muffin tin. Bake for 10-15 minutes, or until lightly browned at the edges. Allow to cool for 5 minutes, then remove and serve warm with fresh mulberry sauce and your favorite vanilla frozen dessert!

6 servings of shortcake and 6 biscuits to freeze

*f you still have frightened moments and wonder at times what the real demands are of this powerful God you once learned about, if you still wonder if it is really safe to let guilt and fear slip away, look closely at this God's "creation" all around you. Could a somber or dangerous Being have engineered something so delightful, amorous and outrageously humorous as the purr in a cat? What sort of humor has to have been the source of the pounce in puppies, the red in roses, the pink in sunsets? What sort of Love the source of caring even in mother reptiles? Whence the majesty in whales and mountains and cedars? Who tie-dyed the fawns, charged the stars, designed the outlandish robes of zebras, tigers and autumn hills? What kind of mirth engineered the duck-billed platypus? What kind of abundance the infinitely variable snowflake? Who micro-engineered the pounding little hearts of scurrying mice?

DANCING HEARTS STRAWBERRY SAUCE

Heart-shaped berry halves in a simple fruit glaze seem to waltz on vanilla ice cream. They definitely do the tango on shortcake!

1	pound	fresh or frozen strawberries
¼	cup	apple juice concentrate or ⅓ cup other concentrated sweetener
¾	cup	apple or apple-strawberry juice
1	tablespoon	arrowroot or kudzu starch or cornstarch

Wash and trim tops off berries; cut each in half. Combine juice concentrate or sweetener with ½ cup of the juice in a medium saucepan; bring to a boil. In a small bowl, dissolve starch in remaining ¼ cup of juice. Mix well again before stirring into boiling liquid; continue to stir until thickened and clear.

Remove from heat and add berries; stir well and allow to sit 3-5 minutes before serving. Add juice to thin if necessary. Serve cold or warm; if you must reheat, do not overcook.

Variation: Substitute ripe, fresh mulberries, blueberries, raspberries or peeled, sliced fresh peaches or apricots.

about 5 cups

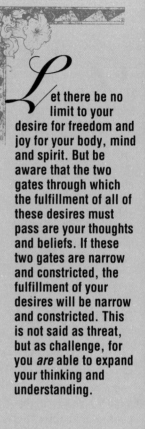

*L*et there be no limit to your desire for freedom and joy for your body, mind and spirit. But be aware that the two gates through which the fulfillment of all of these desires must pass are your thoughts and beliefs. If these two gates are narrow and constricted, the fulfillment of your desires will be narrow and constricted. This is not said as threat, but as challenge, for you *are* able to expand your thinking and understanding.

CRANAPPLE AND CURRANT CRISP

Peel the apples if you wish, but the skins have important elements to offer. Pectin, for example, can help with blood sugar metabolism and lower blood cholesterol levels. This sweet and tart dessert is also a nice accompaniment to natural poultry or game entrees; its joyful rosy color is uplifting with almost any meal!

½	cup	apple juice
½	cup	apple juice concentrate, rice syrup or barley malt
1	cup	currants
2	pounds	baking apples
2	cups	fresh cranberries (if frozen, thaw first)
		extra sweetener, if desired

In a large saucepan, heat juice, ¼ cup of the sweetener and currants to a boil; reduce heat and simmer, covered, while preparing the apples. Core and quarter the apples (peel first if desired), then slice ½-inch thick. Add the apples and cranberries to the simmering currants and stir well; raise heat to high. Bring liquid to a boil, stir, then reduce heat to low and cover. Simmer for about 20 minutes, or until apples are tender but not mushy. Add extra ¼ cup sweetener to taste if desired. Transfer while warm to a large casserole dish or individual serving dishes. Sprinkle generously with Oat-Nut Granola (see p. 143).

*Variation: To bake as a traditional casserole-style crisp or cobbler: Preheat oven to 400°. Soak or simmer currants in liquid and sweetener to plump. In a large mixing bowl, combine currants and liquid with apples and cranberries. Add 2 tablespoons whole wheat pastry flour; stir well. Transfer fruit to a lightly-oiled 9 x 13-inch casserole dish. Spread evenly, then top with **uncooked** oat-nut granola. Cover with foil and bake for 30 minutes; uncover and bake 10-15 minutes longer, or until granola is lightly browned.*

8-10 servings

*I*n response to the preceding paragraph, those who are accustomed to stress the downer side of life will hasten to point out that there are sharks that eat people, and volcanoes and earthquakes, hunger and disease. Look again at what your ego says is hurtful, dear ones. You have it in your power to speed up the day when you know no fear whatsoever— absolutely no fear.

MYSTIC PEAR AND APPLE TOPPING

This warming, soothing sauce owes its magical taste to a combination of two special spices and the gentle flavor of pear. Mace is the lacy covering of the nutmeg seed pod, ground for seasoning use.

Allspice comes from a reddish-brown berry which tastes like a mixture of juniper, cinnamon, nutmeg and clove. If you'd like to use more indigenous seasonings and live in the eastern U.S., learn to identify and harvest the berries of the Common Spicebush, lindera benzoin. Try your own spice blend and enjoy your creation! Good with pancakes or waffles, you might like it as a dessert or snack by itself, served warm or chilled, with oat-nut topping or roasted nuts.

⅓	cup	raisins
⅓	cup	water
⅛	teaspoon	mace
¼	teaspoon	allspice
2	medium	ripe pears
2	medium	apples
½	cup	pear or apple juice
1	teaspoon	arrowroot, kudzu or cornstarch

Combine raisins, water and spices in a medium saucepan. Bring water to a boil; reduce heat to very low and cover; continue to simmer while preparing fruit. Core fruit (peel if desired) and cut in quarters, then slice about ½-inch thick. Add fruit to the simmering currants, stir well and raise heat to bring liquid to a boil again. Cover, reduce heat to low and simmer until fruit is tender but not mushy, about 5-10 minutes. Dissolve starch in juice and stir gently but thoroughly into simmering fruit; continue to stir until starch liquid turns clear. Thin sauce with more juice if necessary.

Quick Variation: Use one of the two fruits instead of both.

Try substituting 1 (16-ounce) can each of water- or juice-packed pears and apples for the fresh fruit, using the drained liquid in place of the water and juice.

Do you know what it's like to be nagged by joy? If not, you have ahead of you the most surprising astonishment you will ever know. You will not always feel high joy, but even when it is absent, it will seem to press, nag and sparkle at you from behind the lattices. You won't quite remember all the details each moment, but you will have a pervading sense that a joy is always surrounding you in what can be thought of as a sort of cosmic mirth. You no longer feel pressed to grasp for it, for you know it stays always near. You know this far beyond any persuasion of mere logic.

OAT-NUT COOKIES OR GRANOLA

Mildly sweet and crispy, these satisfy the cookie urge in a gentle way.

1	cup	rolled oats
1/2	cup	pecans or almonds, finely chopped in a blender or food procesor
1/2	cup	whole wheat pastry flour
3/4	teaspoon	cinnamon, ground
3/4	teaspoon	coriander, ground
1	teaspoon	pure vanilla extract
3	tablespoons	canola oil
1/4	cup	brown rice syrup, maple syrup or honey
2	tablespoons	water (for cookies only)

Preheat oven to 350° for cookies; 300° for granola. Combine all dry ingredients in a mixing bowl; stir well. In a separate bowl, combine liquid ingredients, omitting the water if making granola, and stir well to blend thoroughly. Add liquid mix to dry mix and stir well. Measure 1/8-cup mounds onto an oiled cookie sheet. Using a fork or moistened fingers, flatten each mound to about 1/4-inch thick. Bake 10-15 minutes, or until edges turn light brown. Allow to cool slightly on the sheet pan, then transfer to a cooling rack to cool completely.

For granola, omit the extra liquid and spread mixture evenly across the cookie sheet. Bake for 20 minutes or until golden brown, stirring once after 10 minutes. The granola will seem soft, rather than crunchy, until it has a chance to cool.

Yield: 2 cups granola or 10 cookies

*T*he day comes when there is no longer any need for anyone else's authority to reassure you about your security and well-being in the Universe. You experience absolute well-being and absolute security—sometimes without feeling these at a sensed level. You sense a new kinship with the stars and blue sky. Birds and insects have become your sisters. You no longer try much to understand, for you are occupied in dancing.

COUSCOUS-CURRANT SPICECAKE

A simple way to have your "cake" and fiber, too. No baking required!

4	cups	unfiltered apple juice
½	cup	unsulfured dried currants or raisins
½	cup	whole wheat couscous
1	teaspoon	cinnamon, ground
1	teaspoon	coriander, ground
¼	teaspoon	cloves, ground
¼	teaspoon	nutmeg, ground
1	teaspoon	pure vanilla extract
1	teaspoon	grated rind from organically-grown orange
8-10		mandarin orange sections (optional)

Combine juice and currants in a saucepan over high heat. Bring to a boil, then reduce heat and simmer, covered, for 5 minutes while you measure the spices and couscous into a small bowl and grate the orange rind. Stir couscous and spice mixture into the simmering juice, raise heat and bring to a boil.

Reduce heat to medium and stir well until couscous thickens. Reduce heat to low, cover and simmer 5 more minutes, stirring once halfway through. Remove from heat; stir in vanilla and orange rind. Lightly oil (or rinse with cold water) a 9-inch pie plate; transfer hot couscous mixture to pan, spread evenly and smooth the top with a spoon. Refrigerate until set and completely chilled. Loosen edges with a rubber spatula or knife; transfer cake to a serving platter: place platter upside down over cake and turn over, allowing cake to drop onto platter. Arrange mandarin orange sections on top of cake; top with fruit glaze (see below) or chopped roasted nuts if desired.

Variation: For fruit glaze, heat ¼ cup apple juice to a simmer in a small saucepan, then add, stirring constantly, 1½ teaspoons arrowroot, kudzu or cornstarch dissolved in ¼ cup cold apple juice. Stir and cook over medium heat until juice is thickened and clear. Glaze cake while sauce is warm.

6-10 servings, depending on size of slice

Eventually you will know beyond any whisper of doubt that everything is part of you, is One with you. You will laugh inside as you realize that all creatures together cannot manage to sing all your songs or dance all your dances. Oceans and rivers, clouds and winds and swaying pines will join you, but the chorus will be still too small! All the flowers and gems in the universe can't demonstrate the colors you will feel. You'll know where the wind has been and where it's going, for you were with it all the way. Ah! Be happy, dear One! You have found your Life! You have found what an ancient tradition calls "the marriage bed of God"!

Menus

I AM GENTLE WITH MYSELF, AND ALLOW MY CREATIVE GIFTS TO
EXPRESS WITH JOY!

My eating habits developed over a period of many years: I can be
gentle with myself by changing these habits in a gradual way. As I
strive for deliberate, conscious food habits, I sometimes judge my
actions against the standard of a concept or ideal which is unrealistic
for me. The resultant guilt can be more injurious than the "offending"
behavior, and can intrude upon the learning I might gain from the
experience. What is my body trying to tell me? How can I know
balance if I know nothing of the extremes? So, too with my culinary
"mistakes"...most are edible and full of lessons...*and* Love, if I bless
them with mine! My unique, creative gifts can bring blessings to the
kitchen as I learn to trust and experiment.

MAKING THE MOST OF YOUR TIME IN THE KITCHEN

Regardless of how much "from scratch" cooking you do, your time in the kitchen is valuable. Use it wisely by regularly preparing extra quantities of simple, basic foods which may be used several different ways later. The recipes listed below will allow you to prepare other dishes later without the effort of doing it all "from scratch."

A Simple Salad (salad greens and toppings)

Soaked Almonds or Hazelnuts

Grow Your Own (sprouts)

The Resourceful Pot

The Basic Pot Of Beans

A Simple Pot of Rice (or any grain)

While You Get Sleep

An Ovenful of Simple Veggies

Roasted Garlic

Quinoa-Vegetable Pilaf

Roasted Free-Range Chicken

Roasted Red Pepper Garnish

Any Cooked Pasta

All Salad Dressings

Roasted Sesame Condiment

BREAKFASTS

Actually, any of the recipes in this book may be used to "break the fast". Experiment with your morning habits to see what feels good to you. Be prepared for change; what is balance now may not be balance later. Try all-fruit breakfasts, especially in warm weather, to experience their light, cleansing effect; adding soaked nuts can help this meal carry you through the morning. If you'd like fruit in addition to something a bit more substantial, try eating the fruit by itself an hour or so before the other food to allow it to digest easily. Some people find that eating several pieces of fruit throughout the morning works well. Take advantage of the ever-increasing variety of natural, ready-to-eat whole grain cereals and breads; many are made without super-refined sweeteners and offer a convenient way to eat some of the more unusual grains.

Hot Barley Cereal with Spiced Fruit Compote and Roasted Pecans

Vegetable and Tofu or Egg Frittata
Rosemary and Sage Biscuits with Garlic Essence

Easy Scrambled Tofu with Vegetables
Spiced Roasted Pepitas and Sunflower Seeds

Fruits of Summer Salad with Soaked Hazelnuts

Whole Grain French Toast with Mystic Apple and Pear Topping

Fresh Fruit Smoothie
Blue Corn Pecan Pancakes with Cranberry-Maple Syrup

Honeydew and Canteloupe Melon
(wait 20 minutes)
Baked Sweet Potato with Roasted Pecans and
Easy Cinnamon-Orange Sauce

Garbanzo and Mustard Green Soup
Baked Acorn, Butternut or Buttercup Squash

Sprouted Wheat Toast with Butternut Squash Butter

Spiced Teff with Apricots and Walnuts

When the contemplative experience has come upon you and you have learned to look beyond appearances to the Reality of everything (to "judge just judgments," in the words of a master), you will do much more than just find peace. You will walk in joy! Everything henceforward will be essentially Joy for you. This is ultimate wisdom. No amount of repetition could adequately emphasize this most basic fact of our Reality. You are invited not to talk about this truth, but to experience it.

Your training probably, and your ego certainly, imagine that joy and peace are "out there" somewhere in your future. The truth of the matter, the great wisdom of it, is that they are already with you. How could they not be! Your Nature is Peace and Joy! Just as you are, right now, with all your "faults" and "limitations."

LUNCHES

Salad of Greenleaf Lettuce and Radiccio or Red Cabbage with Shredded
Carrot, Daikon Radish and Sunflower Seeds (see A Simple Salad,
pp. 10-11)
Simple Lemon Vinaigrette
Hearty Japanese Red Bean Stew

Tofu Salad Sandwiches in Whole Wheat Pita Pockets
with Alfalfa Sprouts (see Grow Your Own, p. 19) leaf lettuce and tomato

Salad of Mixed Greens with Stir Fried Natural Beef,
Gold Bell Pepper and Radish
Herbed Apricot-Mustard Dressing

Open-Faced Sandwich of Avocado, Zucchini and
Garlic Spread with Roasted Chicken
Mediterranean Lentil Soup

Watercress, Sweet Potato and Roasted Pecan Salad
Calypso Soup

Spinach and Redleaf Lettuce with Salad of Succotash
Red Pepper Vinaigrette

Caribbean Black Bean and Vegetable Soup
Onion Spelt Bread with Butternut Squash Butter

"Ancient Ones" Burritos with Salsa
Steamed Broccoli

Chicken or Tofu in Clear Broth with Cumin, Red Onion and Cilantro
Dandelion or Curly Endive with Fragrant Potato and Broccoli Salad
(Potato and Broccoli Skillet Hash Variation)

"TLT" Sandwich
Spiced Butternut Squash Soup

DELICIOUS DINNERS

Many of these dishes combine lots of vegetables with whole grains and/or beans or other lean protein sources. As a result, most main dishes, soups, stews, beans and grain or pasta dishes can be served with a salad or vegetable side dish for a complete meal. For those of you who cook for two, all recipes may be prepared in half-sized batches; remember, though, that it often pays to make extra for later use. For those who eat alone, consider sharing meals, preparation and cleanup with a friend or two. Cooking for several doesn't require much more effort than for one, and the shared effort is much more pleasant.

Steamed Vegetable Medley with Couscous
(Quick and Light for a Dancing Heart)
Simple Lemon Vinaigrette
Roasted Sesame Condiment

Spicy Red and Black Bean Tortilla Pie
Mixed Greens with Shredded Carrot and Beet with
Spiced Roasted Pepitas and Sunflower Seeds
Simple Lemon Vinaigrette

Szechuan Stir-Fry with Fresh Asparagus and Sweet Gold Pepper
Long Grain Brown Basmati Rice (see A Simple Pot of Rice, p. 75)
Steamed Carrots (see The Sweet and Simple Ones, p. 43)

Baked Stuffed Sole or Flounder Fillets
Winter Vegetable Braise
Butterhead Lettuce with Simple Lemon Vinaigrette

Quick Tofu, Chicken or Beef Curry (see From Rome to Bombay, p. 113)
Cabbage, Carrot and Cashew Salad with Fresh Cilantro

Roasted Free-Range Chicken with Fresh Herbs and Garlic
Crusty Baked Potatoes with Marjoram, Mushrooms and Leeks
Turnip Greens

Millet Griddlecakes with Mushroom-Garlic Sauce
Braised Brussels Sprouts with Parsley Root

With all this talk of joy, you may wonder if the spiritual life is only joy. The answer is both yes and no. Yes, insofar as you learn to identify with your true Self (the essential content of the "good news" that Jesus and other enlightened masters spoke of—and the only thing this book has been saying). No, in so far as you remain preoccupied with, and therefore blinded by, the daily phenomena and ego values of a perceived separateness which, until deliberately replaced, will keep you from dancing among the stars.

You are invited to a peace and joy and fulfillment in this world beyond anything you can imagine. That's because you live Divine Life and these come as your birthright. They are not things you must somehow go out and acquire; they are your inheritance that awaits within your person to be realized.

Quick Vegetable Sambaar (mixed vegetables version)
Whole Wheat Couscous
Steamed Kale with Lemon Juice and Roasted Sesame Seeds
(Roasted Sesame Condiment, see p. 124)

Simple Broiled Fish
Italian Style Lambsquarters or Spinach with Garlic and Tofu
Simple Baked Potato

Linguini Pasta with Steamed Broccoli, Pinenuts and
Roasted Red Pepper Sauce
Sautéed Rutabagas with Garlic and Chervil

Red Bean and Yellow Squash Chili
Mustard Greens with Almond Butter Sauce
Raw Carrot and Celery Sticks

Brown Rice with Roasted Sesame Condiment
Steamed Kale with Spicy Peanut Sauce
Garlicked Garbanzos with Oregano and Sweet Red Pepper

Whole Grain Macaroni and Cheese with Broccoli, Mushrooms
and Red Bell Pepper
Salad of Romaine Lettuce, Fresh Fennel and Carrot

Gingered Arame with Carrots, Onions and Burdock
Onion-Spelt Bread with Roasted Garlic Spread
Steamed Young Collard Greens with Lemon Juice

FINGER FOODS FOR ENTERTAINING

Marinated Szechuan Tofu Triangles

Spicy Bean Dip with Blue Corn Tortilla Chips

Bonzo Bean Spread with Pita Wedges

*Whole Grain Crackers with Almond Miso Spread
and Daikon Radish Slices*

*Raw Vegetables Platter with Spicy Peanut Dip
(Spicy Peanut Sauce, see p. 103)*

Spiced Roasted Pepitas and Sunflower Seeds

Crispy Brown Rice and Fruit Bars

Oat-Nut Cookies

Blue Corn Pecan Muffins with Butternut Squash Butter

Onion Spelt Bread with Roasted Garlic Spread

Fruit Smoothies

Apple Lemon Cooler

The ancient Rabbi Hillel said something we do well to think about in relationship to our invitation to find our bliss: "If not you, who; if not now, when?" Listen carefully and you will infallibly hear a message in your mind and heart, a message singing forth from the innermost Nature of your shared Life: "Shall we dance?"

PERSONAL CHOICES MAKE A DIFFERENCE

The starting point for sharing unconditional, limitless Love is to respect and nurture ourselves. Whether one has the opportunity for many choices or few, our immediate environment is the area of greatest personal influence. Yet no one lives in a vacuum. We each affect those around us, and the effect of our choices is felt in ways both subtle and potent throughout the universe.

Our food habits are no less significant than others. Agricultural systems use a major portion of the resources of our planet. Increasing population adds to the pressure on our water, soil, fuel and forest resources, and the results of short-sighted management are becoming more evident daily.

Throughout history, wise ones have thought beyond the small view, looking at times to the needs of future generations in deciding how to use precious local resources. Today, with technological arms reaching across the globe in an instant, our personal decisions have greater impact than ever before. It is perhaps not by chance that as we honor ourselves with high quality, balanced nourishment, we contribute to the healing of our planet, as well.

- As you eat locally grown, seasonal foods, much less fuel is used to package and transport food from far away. Pollution related to processing and shipping is reduced significantly. Ultimately, rich soils currently devoted to production of cash crops in hunger-stricken nations may be returned to producing a more indigenous, stable and varied diet for those who live there.

- As you get to know some of the people who produce your food, you help to complete an important circle of communication between yourself and the earth.

- As you eat a widely varied and changing diet, increased personal flexibility and adaptability influences those around you and those around them and those around them and on and on. Crop diversity is encouraged and ecological stability is enhanced. Reliance upon intensive use of increasingly potent chemicals can be lessened in more stable, diverse systems with more natural checks and balances.

- As you eat fewer processed and highly-refined packaged foods, less fuel is used, less water and air polluted.

- As you replace some or all of the animal protein in your diet with complex carbohydrates and vegetable protein, you help to reduce the loss of topsoil and pollution of water associated with energy-intensive methods of livestock production; some land stripped of trees for this purpose may be returned to its natural, life-enhancing forested state.

- As you choose certified organically-grown foods (and animals which have been nourished by them), you help support the natural fertility of our soil, the quality of our water and air, as well as the health and livelihoods of those who invest the extra effort required to grow and harvest them.

J.L.

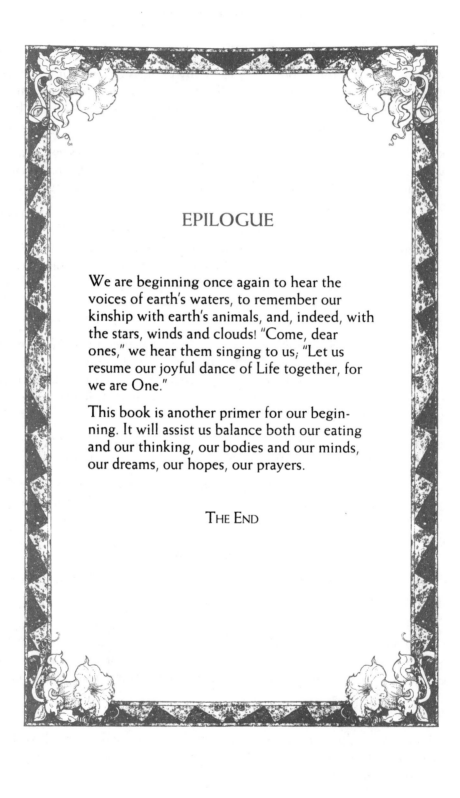

EPILOGUE

We are beginning once again to hear the voices of earth's waters, to remember our kinship with earth's animals, and, indeed, with the stars, winds and clouds! "Come, dear ones," we hear them singing to us; "Let us resume our joyful dance of Life together, for we are One."

This book is another primer for our beginning. It will assist us balance both our eating and our thinking, our bodies and our minds, our dreams, our hopes, our prayers.

THE END

Index